The Trumpet in the Morning

Law and Freedom Today in the
Light of the Hebraeo-Christian Tradition

Stuart Blanch

ARCHBISHOP OF YORK

OXFORD UNIVERSITY PRESS

NEW YORK

Unless otherwise stated, the biblical text used is from *The New English Bible*. © The Delegates of the Oxford University Press and The Syndics of the Cambridge University Press 1961, 1970. Reprinted by permission.

First published in Great Britain in 1979 by Hodder and Stoughton Limited, Mill Road, Dunton Green, Sevenoaks, Kent.

First published in the United States in 1979 by Oxford University Press, New York
Copyright © 1979 by Stuart Blanch

Library of Congress Catalog Card Number 79–896–94

ISBN 0–19–520167–1

Printed in Great Britain by Billing & Sons Limited, Guildford, London and Worcester.

To Brenda
and my family and
to Staff and Students,
past and present, of
Wycliffe Hall, Oxford.

Acknowledgments

I acknowledge my debt to the following, who have knowingly or unknowingly contributed to this enterprise—to the Principal of Wycliffe Hall, Oxford who, by inviting me to give the 1977 Chavasse Lectures, set in train the process of thought which culminated in the writing of this book; to Mr. Edward England of Hodder and Stoughton who encouraged me in it; to Professor Matthew Black and to Sir Norman Anderson, who were kind enough to read the earlier chapters in draft; to many authors and scholars whose writings are quoted here; to Bachman & Turner for the use I have made opposite certain chapters of their *Book of Freedom Quotations*; to Daphne Wood and Val Smith, who between them typed this manuscript; to David Blunt, who assisted me throughout in the production process; and to countless others who, in print and in conversation, have alerted me to the importance of freedom under the law.

Contents

On the third day, when morning came, there were peals of thunder and flashes of lightning, dense cloud on the mountain and a loud trumpet blast; the people in the camp were all terrified.

Moses brought the people out from the camp to meet God, and they took their stand at the foot of the Mountain. Mount Sinai was all smoking because the Lord had come down upon it in fire; the smoke went up like the smoke of a kiln; all the people were terrified, and the sound of the trumpet grew ever louder.

Exodus 19: 16-19 (NEB)

Freedom . . .

The Devil was once asked what he missed most after he was cast out of heaven. He thought for a moment, and replied—"I miss most the sound of the trumpet in the morning." What did the Devil mean, I ask? It is true that he had chosen to reign in hell rather than serve in heaven; he preferred to be a law unto himself instead of an observer of the law of God; he had decided to pursue his own objectives rather than the objectives which God had prescribed for him. In short, he was free. But what did he miss? What was this sound of the trumpet?

Like most men who served in the Forces during the second world war, I did not by any means relish the early call, the fixed routines, the square-bashing, the seemingly irrational regulations, to which we were subject. It represented to me a serious loss of freedom. It was, therefore, a moment of pure delight to pass through the gates on the way home with a pass in my pocket, to change into a suit, to get up when I felt like it and to lounge away the day doing exactly what I wanted to do. But I have to admit that by the end of the week I was secretly glad to climb into uniform again and resume my painful servitude to the ordered life of an R.A.F. station. I missed the sound of the trumpet. I found it onerous to be free. It is experience of this kind, oft repeated and, no doubt, familiar to many of my readers, which lies behind the writing of this book. It is the shadow that flits to and fro across these pages as we study together the issues that arise from the old-age tension between law and freedom.

The more immediate occasion of the book, however, is the serious sense of unease about the future of our own nation, and the seeming erosions of freedom, from which we all suffer and for which we all have our own explanations. The most obvious threat to freedom is represented by the extremist political organisations of the right or the left, and the near-anarchy which is sometimes created thereby on our industrial and political scene. Almost equally obvious is the threat to our freedom posed by the growth of computer techniques which can bank confidential material and make it available at the flick of a switch. The chips are down. The less obvious, but more pervasive, threat, however, is the one posed by a growing disaffection with the processes of law, and a diminishing respect for it. I quote from a pamphlet by Sir Keith Joseph, entitled *Freedom Under the Law* which he wrote in 1975:

> Before I define and analyse the concept of the rule of law, I must point out that historically speaking it is an exotic plant, the exception rather than the rule. England has enjoyed it for three centuries. It was not won without sacrifice; why should we believe that it will sustain itself without any effort on our part? The good things of life are rarely free. A generation back, it seemed as though the whole world were following in our footsteps; all the Victorians took this for granted: Karl Marx was as confident of it as Herbert Spencer, Gladstone as Robert Owen. The preservation of the rule of law was paramount for generation after generation of jurists and political thinkers. By now, we see that the rule of law is a minority taste among the nations of the world. We must earn our continued good fortune. Can our generation consider giving away this birth-right for the very thin stew of "social justice"?

He goes on to say that "law is not as simple as it seems". This book is an attempt to give substance to that artless statement. Indeed, Sir Keith is right—it is not as simple as it seems, and if the point needs any proving, the pages which follow will undoubtedly prove it.

There is a sense in which anyone who attempts a study of this kind is doomed to failure. It requires of him a wide range of knowledge, with which it is unlikely that any one person can be familiar. A writer about "Freedom under the Law" needs to be at the same time, a political philosopher, a jurist, an historian and a moral theologian. And he needs also to be a biblical scholar, insofar as the issue of freedom under the law is extensively treated in the sacred Scriptures, a solid datum of experience which we have to take seriously; the political philosopher, the jurist, the historian and the moral theologian, cannot afford to ignore it. The only contribution I can offer in this field is an examination of the Hebraeo-Christian scriptures with this objective in view—to expose and, if possible, to interpret, a long documentary and theological process which underlies the history of Israel, and bears upon our understanding of freedom and law. That is a modest enough objective, but it is fraught with difficulty, and I entertain little hope of success. And why? Because readers familiar with the subject will be aware that I have failed, in many instances, to prove the point, and readers unfamiliar with it will not think that the point needs proving. And furthermore, to many another reader, the biblical model I have chosen is one to which they owe no loyalty and in which they perceive no particular virtue. But there will be some who share my concern about the erosions of freedom and are not enchanted with the methods sometimes proposed to protect it. There will be some who view the prospect of a certain kind of freedom as a threat to any kind of civilised existence, but have no means of knowing where or how to draw the line. There will be old people, alarmed by the seeming licence of the young, and young people oppressed by the bondage of the old. There will be churchmen lamenting the reassuring disciplines of the past, and radicals burdened with the weight of unchallenged assumptions in the present. And there will be some, more than we might imagine, who are just afraid of what is going to happen on the earth, ready to say to the mountains "fall on us" and to the hills "hide us" (Luke 23: 30):

> Like one, that on a lonesome road
> Doth walk in fear and dread
> And having once turned round walks on
> And turns no more his head:
> Because he knows, a frightful fiend
> Doth close behind him tread.

Altogether, this makes up a goodly company of potential readers who miss the sound of the trumpet in the morning, and wonder why. To them, I apologise in advance for all those glaring omissions, those crude generalisations, those unobserved contradictions, which will no doubt mar this book in your eyes. My only excuse for writing it is that somebody needs to write it.

I do not pretend that this is going to be an easy book to read, because the argument has to rest upon a detailed treatment of biblical material, the meaning of which must always remain uncertain, and continues to produce an unending stream of specialised comment. The confident assertions of the scholars of the last generation are commonly the starting point for a debate by the scholars of the next. The dust gathers in many a second-hand bookshop, and in many a library, on the mortal remains of many a tenaciously-held opinion, now long-since abandoned—at best a useful object of ridicule by the latest Ph.D. aspirant. If this book proves to be useful at all, it will be because it is a serious attempt to make available to those who have to *act,* what others have *thought.* At some point, the professor and the politician, the biblical scholar and the judge, the moral theologian and the parish priest, need to meet each other. In a necessarily limited way, they could meet each other in this book, and the "Considerations" of the last chapter, might help to fructify their conversation. Our freedom is at risk. It has to be preserved in the mind before we can rely on it being preserved in the street. As Sir Keith Joseph said—we who enjoy it still must earn our continued good fortune.

From anarchy
And slavish masterdom alike ...
Preserve my people! Cast not from your walls
All High authority; for where no fear
Awful remains, what mortal will be just?

Aeschylus
Oresteia

The rule of law does not guarantee freedom, since general laws as well as personal edicts can be tyrannical. But increasing reliance on the rule of law clearly played a major role in transforming Western society from a world in which the ordinary citizen was literally subject to the arbitrary will of his master to a world in which the ordinary citizen could regard himself as his own master.

Friedman
Morality and Controls, *New York Times*,
28 October, 1971

. . . Under the Law

Time was when law was the preoccupation of an elect, when judges were sacrosanct and policemen were regarded with alarm or affection, according to your age. As a young man working in Chancery Lane I used occasionally to sit in on a case at the Law Courts in the Strand. It was interesting in an academic way, far from dramatic and seemingly remote from the little world I inhabited. The scene has changed. Policemen are to be seen frequently on our television screens battling with ideologues of one sort or another in the name of "law and order". Chief Constables actually speak to the public. Judges are at risk if they permit themselves little jokes about a coloured man or the National Front. By a not insubstantial minority of the population they are regarded as the lackeys of the establishment, the inflexible guardians of the *status quo* against the forces of free expression and social liberty. The issues are no longer academic, explored within a dusty courtroom, tricked out with the age-old trappings of judicial isolation; they explode in the streets and are debated hotly in many a council chamber and on many a shop floor. The Attorney General is challenged about his relationship to the judiciary. Laws are passed by a slender majority regarding the availability of abortion or family planning advice, to which a substantial minority in the country certainly object on moral grounds. Regulations pile up on top of each other to the point at which the humble citizen is unable to understand them, much less obey them. Thus the law is brought into contempt and everywhere questions arise—by what right do private convictions pass by a small majority into the law of the land? What obligation do we have to obey them when we positively dissent from them? Where is the ordinary citizen to find any genuine recourse against the executive? How can we be sure that the judiciary are not being influenced by or against the party in power?

Consider, too, the question of law as it invades private life, or at least life which has hitherto been regarded as private. Perhaps this is the most sensitive area of concern to twentieth-century man, who feels himself entitled to seek solutions of his personal dilemma in ways of which society has hitherto disapproved, e.g. the use of drugs, the enjoyment of pornography, the dependence on alcohol. Capitalist societies tend to be, in that sense, "permissive", Communist societies are indubitably restrictive—there are no "private" acts to which the state can be indifferent. Such questions, however, large and menacing though they undoubtedly are, beg *the* question which is—what is law and what is its status in society and in the life of the individual?

Our misfortune is that in English we use one word "law" to represent a huge variety of meanings. It can mean anything from a law about parking on double yellow lines or driving on the left, to fire precautions in offices or safety regulations in factories. It can command you to send your child to this school rather than to that. It restricts the amount of money you may take out of the country; it may cause you to think in terms of millimetres rather than inches. These are, no doubt, very important matters but hardly of the kind to win unquestioning moral assent. At the other end of the spectrum law can stand for an expression of the underlying ground plan of the universe, physical and spiritual, which carries with it sanctions infinitely more impressive than conviction in a court of law or imprisonment. To infringe law in that sense is a kind of death. It burdens the conscience, it cries out for forgiveness. In between these two extremes you can impart to the term "law" almost any meaning you choose. The English, therefore, start at a serious disadvantage in comparison with the Hebrews who enjoy a wide range of nomenclatures for what we unthinkingly call law.

But it is not just a question of nomenclature, the idea of law has a long philosophical history behind it. By way of example I refer to an unpublished paper by Sir Norman Anderson, formerly director of the Institute of Advanced Legal Studies in the University of London. It is entitled "The Concept of Law" and was delivered to a specialist audience. He distinguishes "in regard to law in the secular sense" no less than six schools of thought still influential in our own day, viz. the Imperative school, the Kelsonian school, the Historical school, the Sociological school, the American Realists school, the Swedish Realists school.

Professor Anderson prefixes this paragraph with the words "law in the secular sense"—which provokes the important question to which this book is largely addressed, viz. how far is it possible in our present stage of development to arrive at an acceptable definition of law exclusively in a secular sense? Law down the ages, for better or for worse, has for the most part been associated inextricably with morality and religion. The Code of Hammurabi, one of the earliest extant codes dating from the second millennium B.C., has in its prologue a description of the King's piety and his care for the worship of the gods. It seems that law habitually carries with it supernatural sanctions. This is borne out elsewhere in his paper by Sir Norman's comment on Muslim law—"There is no room in Islamic thought for any concept of natural law but only for a law which was basically both divine and revealed." Secular law therefore, if we may thus describe it, has a relatively short history and is unlikely on the basis of so restricted a model to be able to offer as yet any convincing rationale for itself. It is too early to tell whether law devoid of supernatural sanctions can monitor and sustain a civilisation which has, in whatever sense we use the term, religious foundations.

In search of a larger model, therefore, I turn to a source more accessible to most of us than the ancient Code of Hammurabi, enlightened and comprehensive though it is, or the majestic edifice of Muslim law in which Sir Norman is expert. Our source can hardly be other than one which has largely formed not only our jurisprudence but our attitude to law in general. I refer, of course, to the law of the Hebrews, itself a substantial corpus of law with a history of nearly four thousand years behind it. It is indeed a large model in every sense which must command the attention if no longer the assent of western democracy. For practical purposes we shall be confining our attention to that process of development which took place within the period covered roughly by Holy Scripture. My Jewish friends would no doubt regard this as a quite arbitrary act of selection, given the long, unceasing processes in which that law has been elaborated and refined down the ages since the beginning of the Christian era. But for all its refinements in detail the general attitude to the law which prevails in orthodox Judaism today has not substantially changed. It could hardly be better put than in this passage from *The Pentateuch and Haftorah* published by Soncino.

> Amid this spiritual confusion and moral chaos, Judaism remains clear-eyed and unmoved. It clings unswervingly to the Divine origin of the Decalogue; and continues to proclaim that there is an everlasting distinction between right and wrong, an absolute "Thou shalt" and "Thou shalt not" in human life, a categorical imperative in religion— high above the promptings of passion, the peradventure of inclination, or the fashion of the hour. Weak and erring man needs an authoritative code in matters of right and wrong, laying down with unmistakable clearness the chief heads of duty, and denouncing the chief classes of sins. Such a Divine affirmation of the Moral Law was at all times a vital necessity for mankind, in order to set aside doubt, and to silence that perverse casuistry which is always ready to call good evil, and evil good. God is not only our Father. He is also our Law-giver; and in the Decalogue, He has made known to the children of men the foundations on which human welfare and happiness can be built.

The least that can be said about this passage is that we know where we stand; and who would not applaud so confident a stance sustained through centuries of migration and persecution, of subjection and contempt? But is it true? This is a question which ought not to be evaded even by those for whom this particular moral and religious stance is *de facto* wholly alien. They do not believe in God, they do not believe in the God of the Hebrews, they do not believe in an unchanging moral imperative, but they can hardly deny that this view of life exists, that it has had a long history, that it is certain of a long future, that it underlies many of our attitudes, social and personal, and undoubtedly forms the basis of law as we at present experience it in the western hemisphere. Secularise some of those expressions if you like—"a Divine origin ... moral law ... God is our Father", dispel the clouds from the summit of Sinai, close your ears to the voice, bury the tablets of stone, and we are still left with a solid ineffaceable deposit on the face of the earth, viz. the life and religion of Israel, mirrored in a thousand synagogues, perpetuated in architecture and song and literature and at the heart of it all—law. I make this point because I would not wish the would-be reader to discount the main thesis of this book merely because he does not share in the Hebraeo-Christian tradition, or to grow unnecessarily impatient with the rather arcane theological pursuits I am about to engage in. Confusions regarding the law, not only in its operation, but in its very essence, abound. If law, however, is to be regarded as a corner-stone of civilisation as we have come to experience it, then no responsible person, whether he be Jew, Christian, Muslim or atheist, can rest easy with this confusion. It erodes confidence in our social processes, it breeds extremists and threatens the happiness and well-being of millions of our fellow countrymen. "Secular law" has, as I have said, too short a life-span to be a reliable model. Let us begin, therefore, with a model which has the virtue of antiquity, coherence and solidity, and has manifestly produced a measure of "human welfare and happiness". We may have to discard the model but we need to understand it if we are to put in its place another model of equal significance and weight. I make no apologies, therefore, for launching on what is bound to be an exacting voyage which will require a certain orientation of mind, and some knowledge of the historical and theological structures within which the Hebrew model came into being and gradually acquired the totality which it represents today.

But if the reader who is not part of the Hebraeo-Christian tradition has to make room in his mental scenery for the law, as it is explicated within that tradition, the Jew and the Christian also may have adjustments to make. A certain amount of scene-shifting may be necessary, which could make the stage look strangely different. As that tradition comes down to us in translation we experience again the difficulty to which I alluded earlier in this chapter—and it is a linguistic one. The Books of Moses (from Genesis to Deuteronomy) are commonly called The Books of the Law. And to us law conjures up all that is in the end disagreeable, restrictive, minatory. A famous example is provided for us in John Bunyan's *Pilgrim's Progress*.

> FAITHFUL. ... So soon as the man overtook me, he was but a word and a blow, for down he knocked me, and laid me for dead. But when I was a little come to myself again, I asked him wherefore he served me so? He said, because of my secret inclining to Adam the First; and with that he struck me another deadly blow on the breast, and beat me down backward: so I lay at his foot as dead as before. So, when I came to myself again, I cried him mercy; but he said, I know not how to show mercy; and with that he knocked me down again. He had doubtless made an end of me, but that one came by, and bid him forbear.
>
> CHRISTIAN. Who was that that bid him forbear?
>
> FAITHFUL. I did not know him at first; but as he went by I perceived the holes in his hands and his side; then I concluded that he was our Lord. So I went up the hill.
>
> CHRISTIAN. That man that overtook you was Moses. He spareth none, neither knoweth he how to show mercy to those that transgress his law.

Of course law can become just a burden, it can forget "how to show mercy to those that transgress", but to the pious Israelite of an earlier era the law was a joy, not a burden—"I have had as great delight in the way of thy testimonies as in all manner of riches." That quotation from Psalm 119 itself reveals the difficulty. The Hebrews had many words for law; we have one, and our word is a singularly inadequate word for what the Hebrews understood to be the gift of God at Sinai. The Books of Moses are more rightly represented as Torah, i.e. the teaching of God. The picture is not so much of

a stern judge handing down judgments and imposing fearful
penalties as of a father teaching his child how to walk and
what to eat and how to avoid danger, introducing him to new
truths, opening his eyes to the stately ordering of the universe.

> When Israel was a boy, I loved him; I called my
> son out of Egypt. It was I who taught Ephraim
> to walk, I who had taken them in my arms; but
> they did not know that I harnessed them in
> leading-strings and led them with bonds of love—
> that I had lifted them like a little child to my cheek,
> that I had bent down to feed them. (Hos. 11: 1-3)

Dr. Whitehouse in his article in *Theological Word Book of
the Bible* makes the same point—"the law was, in the first
instance, an offer of life after a prescribed and blessed
pattern. To men who cannot, or will not, accept what is
offered in this Word of God it becomes a stern command."

The misunderstanding of the word "law" in English is
compounded by a similar confusion about the meaning of
nomos in the Greek New Testament. Like our word law,
nomos has to do service for a wide range of meanings. Kitell's
Theological Dictionary of the New Testament has this to
say—"the word Nomos in ancient times has a comprehensive
range of meaning which embraces any kind of existing or
accepted norm, order, custom, usage or tradition. The concept
is religious in origin and plays a main role in the cultus ... as
political order developed in Greece, however, the word came
into specialised use in the juridical sphere." Little surprise
then that St. Paul, captured in an inadequate terminology,
should have been regarded as one who habitually set the
Gospel over against the law and inveighed against law as a
means of salvation. Yes indeed, but the law is, and remains,
"holy and good".

We all have some scene-shifting to do, atheists, Jews and
Christians, if we are to recover any sense of the weight and
importance of law in the life of society and of the individual.
We need not range ourselves on opposite sides in this
particular matter, guarding our belief or our unbelief. We
just need to have the long-term good of mankind at heart and
desire for it "its human welfare and happiness". My stance

will be obvious as the book proceeds, but I do not require that others should accept it. My only hope is that I shall have shown that we cannot lightly dismiss that great deposit of law and custom, of aspiration and attitude, which at its best we find within the Hebraeo-Christian tradition. I do not ask that you shall worship *my* God before you can welcome *a* law of God everywhere at work sustaining the moral and physical universe and calling us to glad co-operation—a way of blessedness and truth.

And the words for Freedom are prophecies.

Levi
Christmas Sermon from *Death is a Pulpit*

They lie by the way in the shadow of death,
But they fell with their face to the morning.

Waddell

Prophets

I am proceeding on the assumption that law in our present condition is essential to any ordering of corporate life that can legitimately be called "civilisation". The only alternatives to the rule of law are anarchy or tyranny. The question is, therefore, how, and on what basis, is law to be restored to its proper role as guardian of the weak against the strong and of the individual against the collective? To ask this question is silently to acknowledge the fact that secular law, i.e. law divorced from its supernatural origins has yet to prove itself. That is why we are looking at a particular model, i.e. Hebrew law, which is historically associated with Western civilisation and underlies many of its characteristic institutions. The reader may well object to this procedure on two grounds:

1. that there seems little reason for using law, as understood by an unimportant Semitic clan, as a model, and
2. that the circumstances under which that law grew up and was administered three thousand years ago, are vastly different from our present multi-national, multi-religious, multi-cultural civilisation of today.

So may I attend to these objections for a moment? It is agreed straightaway that even in its most successful period, Israel comprised a tiny nation, a small pebble on a large beach, amidst the mighty nations of the ancient world. But unless we are trapped in the odd assumption that "big" equals "important", we have at least to allow for the possibility, if no more, that Israel was a "peculiar people". This conviction has certainly sustained their identity as a nation through the best part of four thousand years, and it is based on the prior conviction that the law they received at Sinai was a law intended for the whole world. Western man confronted with that claim is apt to blow a fuse. Replace the fuse and try again. We owe mathematics to the Egyptians, philosophy to the Greeks, jurisprudence to the Romans, astronomy to Babylon—or roughly so. Is it too much to believe that there was entrusted to Israel the solemn task of creating a foundation of law on which "human welfare and happiness" for all could be built? This is what they believed at 1,000 B.C.; this is what they believe today. We just have to allow for the fact that they could be right. The second objection arises from the curious impression prevalent in the late twentieth century that there is something about the twentieth century which makes it discontinuous with the past—as if we had a monopoly of knowledge and a vested interest in change. Of course the face of the earth, and those relatively small areas which man actually inhabits, has changed—although its artefacts are not as impressive as we might suppose. We travel faster, our plumbing, on the whole, is better and our computers have some advantages over the ancient abacus. But we are still part of a homogeneous civilisation going well back behind the history of the Hebrews, in which money is the accepted means of exchange, in which war is an instrument of policy and in which we enjoy the developing products of technology. The world did not suddenly become "modern" with the invention of the internal combustion engine, or heavier-than-air flight. The Japanese contingent on the Nile today has something to learn from those who built the pyramids. Some of the glass work of the ancient world remains still beyond the capacity of the modern world. On the whole, murder and theft and false witness are still regarded by the majority as undesirable as they seemed to be to the ancient Hebrews in the desert of Sinai. A society such as ours, with its seemingly insoluble social problems, can hardly afford to ignore the social and communal wisdom of the past, however remote it may seem. We need all the friends we can get. You may still disagree, but I hope I have shown that it is not entirely unreasonable to appeal to the model I have suggested.

There would be many ways of studying the Hebrew model but I start on the well-founded educational principle that we begin with what we know rather than with what we can only surmise. In fact we know a great deal—much more than one might suppose from the uncritical reading of popular books about the Bible, or uncritical viewing of the helpful, but sometimes tendentious, documentaries on the television screen. I choose, therefore, to begin with the extremely well-documented, thoroughly researched period of Hebrew history which we call the monarchy. It covers a period of about five hundred years from its inauguration until its demise. This particular period of history is described and reflected in what is called, in the Hebrew Bible, the second canon, i.e. all those documents comprising Joshua, Judges, I and II Samuel, I and II Kings and all the prophets. In the Oxford Study Bible, which I am using, this represents 497 double-column pages of English text which may, where necessary, be supplemented by the two books of Chronicles, themselves accounting for another seventy-one pages. I hope I am right in thinking (though it is difficult to prove) that this is the most thorough and detailed contemporary presentation of a period of ancient history which is extant today. We are not, therefore, dealing with myths or fancies, or later reconstructions, but with material regarded by the authors themselves as sober history. It is the history of a society unique in the ancient world which is, nominally at least, articulated on a basis of obedience to a law regarded as having been received from God and sustained by Divine authority. This is sufficiently unusual in itself to merit examination. It could be that the history of this peculiar people remains peculiarly important for mankind as a whole, and for twentieth-century western civilisation in particular.

The reader needs to understand that the Hebrew Bible is divided into three so-called canons—the Torah, the prophets and the writings—and in that sense the Hebrew Bible is markedly different from our own, which is in a different order, following the Greek revision of the Old Testament dating from the first century B.C. The documents we are considering, therefore, comprise "the prophets" and they fall into two distinct categories. What we tend to designate as history is called the "former prophets"; what we designate as prophets is called the "latter prophets". It will, I hope, become obvious why this should be so later in the course of the argument.

An indirect testimony is sometimes more convincing than a

direct testimony. I turn, therefore, first of all to the latter prophets who often unconsciously reflect the circumstances under which their society was living. History emerges from their writings in an incomplete and haphazard way, rather than by deliberate intention. The names of the kings, the earthquakes, the wars, the plagues, the international agreements, commercial practices and religious observance, appear in their writings as they might appear in a casual private letter or a speech in parliament. This is indirect testimony of the highest value. The prophets were reacting to their world and reacting in a highly significant way. They indeed have spiritual links with a perfectly familiar feature of the ancient world, viz. the cultic prophets—who foretold the future, presided at religious functions, were subject to fits and trances and were regarded with a mixture of awe and amusement by the populace. Like the gurus and ecstatics of today, they commanded, although they did not always deserve, attention. But the Hebrew prophets far transcended their origins. One of them, Amos, even went so far as to disown any connection with them. They stood for, and never ceased to proclaim, a particular interpretation of the nature of man and of man's existence here on earth. They believed in an unchanging moral order which underlay not only the life of the individual but the life of the kingdom and the cosmos. The stars moved in accordance with this unbending order, and men prospered or failed on the basis of their obedience to, or neglect of, that moral order.

> Can horses gallop over rocks?
> Can the sea be ploughed with oxen?
> Yet you have turned into venom the process of law
> and justice itself into poison,
> you who are jubilant over a nothing and boast,
> "Have we not won power by our own strength?"
> O Israel, I am raising a nation against you, and
> they shall harry your land from Lebo-hamath to
> the gorge of the Arabah.
> This is the very word of the Lord God of Hosts.
> (Amos 6: 12-14)

There is a curious consonance about the law that rules in

Heaven and the law that rules on earth. When you come to think of it, this is an extraordinary phenomenon and cries out for explanation. The prophets were separated from each other both by time and by locality. Few of them knew each other, and it is not certain that any of them were familiar with the recorded utterances of any other. Yet under a bewildering variety of cirumstances, political, social and personal, they believed and proclaimed the same message. Where did they get it from? How did they receive it? Their testimony to themselves was that they spoke the inspired Word of God—to match the particular crises in national or international affairs which called for their intervention. At that level they sometimes disagreed with each other, or so it seems to us. Elisha's political stance was rather different from Elijah's. Isaiah confidently foretold the preservation of Jerusalem. Jeremiah equally confidently foretold its destruction. Some valued the temple and its cult; some distinctly did not. One prophet was to be heard counselling the Hebrew exiles in Babylon to settle down; another was to be heard telling them not to settle down. The prophets were, in the best sense of the term, "opportunists", unwilling to be governed by precedents, always looking for the contemporary relevant word. But for all these variations in style, temperament, circumstance and expectation, they were at one in proclaiming the majesty and relevance of the law of God in everyday affairs. This will hardly surprise many of my readers because they have always taken this for granted, but anyone who is familiar with biblical scholarship over the last three hundred years, will know that it is surprising. Perhaps I ought to say why.

In the Oxford Honours School of Theology, the following question used occasionally to be asked—"Did Hosea know the Ten Commandments?" Pupils were advised never to attempt it unless they had nothing else to attempt, because the question, harmless though it seems, calls for a wide-ranging knowledge of scripture and the controversies which have arisen from it. However well the examinee answers the question, he will have left a great deal out. He will get beta minus if he is lucky. There was a time when it was widely believed that the prophets were themselves, under God's inspiration, the creators of that mighty ethico/legal system which will for ever be associated with Judaism; that concern with justice so characteristic of later Judaism sprang from a fruitful interaction between the prophets and the social circumstances to which they addressed themselves. But times have changed, and it is now permitted to ask—did Hosea know the Ten Commandments? For if he did, the prophets must be seen not as innovators, or as creators of law, but rather as the exponents of it. Yes, Hosea did know the Ten Commandments, and they are quoted in the writings attributed to him.

> Hear the word of the Lord, O people of Israel;
> for the Lord has a controversy with the inhabitants
> of the land.
> There is no faithfulness or kindness,
> and no knowledge of God in the land;
> there is swearing, lying, killing, stealing, and
> committing adultery;
> they break all bounds and murder follows murder.
> Therefore the land mourns, and all who dwell in it
> languish,
> and also the beasts of the field,
> and the birds of the air;
> and even the fish of the sea are taken away.
> (Hos. 4: 1-3 RSV)

As you will observe, the commandments are not in the familiar order, but are, without reasonable doubt, reminiscent of what we call the Decalogue. The Decalogue was the central part of the so-called Torah, i.e. the Books of Moses. The word Torah occurs forty-nine times in the prophetic writings, e.g. Give ear to the Torah of our God (Isaiah); they did not walk in the Torah (Jeremiah); the priests have violated the Torah (Ezekiel); they have despised the Torah of the Lord (Amos); the Torah shall go forth from Zion (Micah); remember the Torah of Moses (Malachi). The prophets were not plucking denunciations and precepts from the sky; they were applying the known Torah of God to flagrant abuses of it that they observed in their society. Thus it was that they stood before kings, remonstrating with them on their failure to keep the Torah of God. Here is a classic expression of an age-old theme.

> The Lord sent Nathan the prophet to David, and when he entered his presence, he said to him, "There were once two men in the same city, one rich and the other poor. The rich man had large flocks and herds, but the poor man had nothing of his own except one little ewe lamb. He reared it himself, and it grew up in his home with his own sons. It ate from his dish, drank from his cup and nestled in his arms; it was like a daughter to him. One day a traveller came to the rich man's house, and he, too mean to take something from his own flocks and herds to serve his guest, took the poor man's lamb and served up that." David was very angry, and burst out, "As the Lord lives, the man who did this deserves to die! He shall pay for the lamb four times over, because he has done this and shown no pity." Then Nathan said to David, "You are the man. This is the word of the Lord the God of Israel to you: 'I anointed you king over Israel, I rescued you from the power of Saul, I gave you your master's daughter and his wives to be your own, I gave you the daughters of Israel and Judah; and, had this not been enough, I would have added other favours as great. Why then have you flouted the word of the Lord by doing what is wrong in my eyes? You have struck down Uriah the Hittite with the sword; the man himself you murdered by the sword of the Ammonites, and you have stolen his wife.' " (II Sam. 12: 1-9)

David had committed two offences against the Torah—murder and adultery. And here is another example.

> Naboth of Jezreel had a vineyard near the palace of Ahab king of Samaria. One day Ahab made a proposal to Naboth: "Your vineyard is close to my palace; let me have it for a garden; I will give you a better vineyard in exchange for it or, if you prefer,

its value in silver." But Naboth answered, "The Lord forbid that I should let you have land which has always been in my family." So Ahab went home sullen and angry because Naboth would not let him have his ancestral land. He lay down on his bed, covered his face and refused to eat. His wife Jezebel came in to him and said, "What makes you so sullen and why do you refuse to eat?" He told her, "I proposed to Naboth of Jezreel that he should let me have his vineyard at its value or, if he liked, in exchange for another; but he would not let me have the vineyard." "Are you or are you not king in Israel?" said Jezebel. "Come, eat and take heart; I will make you a gift of the vineyard of Naboth of Jezreel." So she wrote a letter in Ahab's name, sealed it with his seal and sent it to the elders and notables of Naboth's city, who sat in council with him. She wrote: "Proclaim a fast and give Naboth the seat of honour among the people. And see that two scoundrels are seated opposite him to charge him with cursing God and the king, then take him out and stone him to death." So the elders and notables of Naboth's city, who sat with him in council, carried out the instructions Jezebel had sent them in her letter: they proclaimed a fast and gave Naboth the seat of honour, and these two scoundrels came in, sat opposite him and charged him publicly with cursing God and the king. Then they took him outside the city and stoned him, and sent word to Jezebel that Naboth had been stoned to death.

As soon as Jezebel heard that Naboth had been stoned and was dead, she said to Ahab, "Get up and take possession of the vineyard which Naboth refused to sell you, for he is no longer alive; Naboth of Jezreel is dead." When Ahab heard that Naboth was dead, he got up and went to the vineyard to take possession. (I Kings 21: 1-17)

Four offences against the Torah are denounced—coveting, false witness, **murder**, theft. And here is another example which cannot but raise an echo in the heart of many a social reformer who observes, even if he does not describe it as such, a flagrant breach of the Torah of God.

> Listen to this, you who grind the destitute and plunder the humble, you who say, "When will the new moon be over so that we may sell corn? When will the sabbath be past so that we may open our wheat again, giving short measure in the bushel and taking overweight in the silver, tilting the scales fraudulently, and selling the dust of the wheat; that we may buy the poor for silver and the destitute for a pair of shoes?" (Amos 8: 4-6)

The prophets, of course, were not casuists, applying a regulation here, making a point there, binding heavy burdens on the poor; rather they were radical exponents of the law, requiring obedience to it not in the letter but in the spirit, pouring scorn on those who kept the sabbath in the letter but were eager for it to be over so that they could get back to exploiting the people again. The Torah of God was not something written on two tablets of stone, to be honoured by conventional observance, but to be a matter of heart and will. The prophets always held out the hope that in the end God would put his Torah into the heart of the people.

We ought not to be surprised to hear the prophets described as radical interpreters of the law. There is a sense in which Samuel, for example, stands as the fountain head of both law and prophecy. "He was established to be a prophet in Israel", and that is true. But it is also true that he was accepted and honoured as a judge.

> Samuel acted as judge in Israel as long as he lived, and every year went on circuit to Bethel and Gilgal and Mizpah; he dispensed justice at all these places, returning always to Ramah. That was his home and the place from which he governed Israel, and there he built an altar to the Lord. (I Sam. 7: 15-17)

Here then was a prophet applying the law of God to the

complex and, no doubt, tiresome personal and community disputes of his day. He did not pluck his judgments out of the sky; he consulted the Torah of God in a book. To say this, therefore, of the prophet is not in any way to diminish his stature, it is rather to set him against a background of law, more articulate and detailed than we might have supposed. Their testimony is all the more powerful for being unintended. They were not, as a historian or a jurist might be, out to prove anything; the information we receive from them is by the way. Their majestic concept of justice as the abiding principle of the whole created universe ("Let justice roll on like a river, and righteousness like an ever-flowing stream" Amos 5: 24), is not just a concept; it is a practical resource, the way of blessedness and peace, a guarantee of social order, an expression of God's love and concern for the world. Vastly different though they were from each other, in temperament and circumstance, they were united in this, that God had given their people a law which was to be not only for Israel but for all mankind. They strove with might and main to naturalise this law in the life of their contemporaries, to make it effective in the affairs of men. Politicians and priests, kings and commoners, natives and aliens, were to live in obedience to it and find therein a way of blessedness and peace. The attitude of the prophets is cogently described in the following passage from Kitell's *Theological Dictionary* Vol IV, p. 1039:

> Prophetic preaching rests on a new encounter with God and on the breaking of this divine reality into the pious, yet ungodly activity of the people. Not a new idea of God, but a new encounter with God, is the essence and basis of prophetic preaching. This enables us to understand the attitude of the prophets towards the Law. They do not think that they have to tell the people what God requires for the first time. Their preaching of repentance presupposes that man has been told already what is good, and what the Lord his God requires of him (Mi. 6: 8). The prophets often formulate the divine will in a new way. They often bring out new features. But they neither have nor do they seek to arouse the sense of posing a hitherto unknown demand.

Indeed, prophetic preaching recognises not merely the Law but also its basis. Israel is the divinely chosen people. (Am. 2: 9; 3: 2; Is. 1: 2; Hos. 8: 13 f.). Violation of the Law is apostasy from Yahweh (Is. 1: 27 f.). The prophets always condemn infringements of the commandments (Am. 5: 7, 10 ff.; Hos. 5: 10; 4: 2; Jer. 7: 9). Hos. 8: 12 expressly presupposes a written law.

The prophets had many functions and our spiritual debt to them is enormous, but amongst their gifts to posterity none is more important than their belief in the unchanging law of God as the only basis for a just and humane society. We do not always recognise our debt to them, we who would heal the wounds of our people lightly.

Liberty is conforming to the majority.

Hugh Scanlon
BBC Television, 9 August, 1977

Liberty is when I am allowed to defy Mr. Scanlon.

Paul Johnson
BBC Television, 9 August, 1977

IV

Kings

The "latter prophets" as they are known in the Hebrew canon, bear witness without ever intending to do so to the existence of a "law" which was known to their contemporaries and was, even in the breach of it, regarded as authoritative. I myself regarded this with whatever qualifications in particular cases, as proven. The prophets were not creators of the ethico/legal system of Israel, but penetrating and radical exponents of it. Its very authority in the eyes of the people rested upon the assumption that law was the creation of God and had been committed to his chosen people in the phenomena of fire and thunder and smoke at Sinai. In the ark, at the centre of the cult, were two tablets of stone containing ten words pronounced by God at dictation speed. This is the assumption shared by the prophets themselves and those to whom they spoke. We turn now to examine this assumption in the light of the history of the period, known in the sacred canon as the "former prophets", viz. the Books of Joshua, Judges, I and II Samuel, I and II Kings.

Certain points will arise straightaway in the mind of the reader regarding the former prophets. I refer to two such:

1. Why should this particular corpus of literature, assumed by us who are readers of the English Bible, to be history, be called "prophecy" in the Hebrew Bible? Strangely enough it is an obvious question largely ignored by experts in the field, often dealt with in a mere aside or a footnote, or a paragraph in a learned paper. It could be because there is a sense in which Samuel is the dominant figure in this particular period who emerges out of the situation described in Joshua/Judges and is responsible for the direction which history subsequently took. Samuel occupies twenty-four chapters of narrative—

second only to Moses, therefore, in importance, if the literary remains of Israel are any evidence. And Samuel was a prophet. It could be indeed that parts of the narrative derive directly from him. It is not too difficult, therefore, to see why this particular corpus of literature should be called "prophetic".

2.   Another explanation is that the period described in I and II Samuel and I and II Kings corresponds roughly to what was known as the "prophetic era", i.e. the period from the founding of the monarchy to its demise nearly five hundred years later. The term "prophetic era" is surely significant. It would not require a very diligent reader of Scripture to discover that there is a certain coinherence between prophet and king. They are often seen together in the streets and the gardens, in the mountains and on the battlefields of Israel. How well I remember a hot, dusty afternoon in Jerusalem viewing, with the aid of a friendly rabbi, the precise location of Isaiah's house in relation to the "king's garden". Prophecy, allowing for a few chronological rough edges, is largely coextensive with the period of the monarchy. Perhaps we shall see why this should be so later, but for the moment it could be a possible explanation of how this particular period of history, and the writing related to it, should be regarded as "prophetic".

There could be many other explanations; there may indeed be no explanation at all. It could be that prophetic writings and the historical writings were kept in the same cupboard in some literary genizah somewhere. Nevertheless, theologically if not historically this association of the prophets and history is of the utmost importance and I shall hope to show why. The tablets of stone play a silent but important role in both.

It is sometimes asserted for good respectable reasons that the Book of Deuteronomy ought to be seen not as the last Book of the Pentateuch but as the first book of the prophets. It is an attractive hypothesis because Moses would then be seen not simply as the great liberator and law giver but as the prophet he undoubtedly was, looking out across the Plains of Pisgah seeing the future history of Israel in perspective, viewing long ahead of time the coming monarchy, the coming exile, the world role of Israel, the birth of Christ and the salvation of all mankind—a vision indeed worthy of one who was not only a prophet but the friend of God.

> There has never yet risen in Israel a prophet like Moses, whom the Lord knew face to face: remember all the signs and portents which the Lord sent him to show in Egypt to Pharaoh and all his servants and the whole land; remember the strong hand of Moses and the terrible deeds which he did in the sight of all Israel. (Deut. 34: 10-12)

But one has to say that there is no documentary evidence for putting Deuteronomy among the prophets. It stubbornly retains its place in the Torah, so I have no alternative but to begin with the Books that follow it. I need not detain you long with the Book of Joshua more than just to draw your attention to what we might call the "keynote" speech at the beginning.

> After the death of Moses the servant of the Lord, the Lord said to Joshua son of Nun, his assistant, "My servant Moses is dead; now it is for you to cross the Jordan, you and this whole people of Israel, to the land which I am giving them. Every place where you set foot is yours: I have given it to you, as I promised Moses. From the desert and the Lebanon to the great river, the river Euphrates, and across all the Hittite country westwards to the Great Sea, all this shall be your land. No one will ever be able to stand against you: as I was with Moses, so will I be with you; I will not fail you or forsake you. Be strong, be resolute; it is you who are to put this people in possession of the land which I swore to give to their fathers. Only be strong and resolute; observe diligently all the law which my servant Moses has given you. You must not turn from it to right or left, if you would prosper wherever you go. This book of the law must ever be on your lips; you must keep it in mind

day and night so that you may diligently observe all
that is written in it. Then you will prosper and be
successful in all that you do." (Joshua 1: 1-10)

Whatever may be the factual history of this "Book of the
Law" (and there is a huge diversity of opinion on this matter)
the author of Joshua is clear in what he wishes to say. He
wishes to say that leadership in Israel now devolving upon
Joshua is forever associated with guardianship of and
obedience to the law of God.

> At that time Joshua built an altar to the Lord the
> God of Israel on Mount Ebal. The altar was of
> blocks of undressed stone on which no tool of iron
> had been used, following the commands given to the
> Israelites by Moses the servant of the Lord, as is
> described in the book of the law of Moses. At the
> altar they offered whole-offerings to the Lord, and
> slaughtered shared-offerings. There in the presence
> of the Israelites he engraved on blocks of stone a
> copy of the law of Moses. And all Israel, elders,
> officers, and judges, took their stand on either side
> of the Ark, facing the levitical priests who carried
> the Ark of the Covenant of the Lord—all Israel,
> native and alien alike. Half of them stood facing
> Mount Gerizim and half facing Mount Ebal, to
> fulfil the command of Moses the servant of the
> Lord that the blessing should be pronounced first.
> Then Joshua recited the whole of the blessing and
> the cursing word by word, as they are written in
> the book of the law. There was not a single word of
> all that Moses had commanded which he did not
> read aloud before the whole congregation of Israel,
> including the women and dependants and the aliens
> resident in their company. (Joshua 8: 30-35)

The parallel with Nehemiah 8, verses 1-12 will be obvious to
any of you who like to look at the passage. Whatever the
implications of that parallel (and they are many and they are
very obscure) the Book of Joshua in its present form includes
a passage which roundly asserts the responsibility of a leader

in Israel for ensuring obedience to the law of God (on two Tablets of Stone) as the condition of Israel's national life.

Genesis refers to Torah once, Exodus seven times, Leviticus sixteen times, Numbers nine times, Deuteronomy twenty-two times, Joshua eight times but Judges not at all. Instead the Book of Judges describes with a wealth of interesting and sometimes amusing detail, the condition of the early Israelite settlers in Canaan and summarises the whole period of history in a somewhat peremptory way by saying that—"in those days there was no king in Israel, everyone did that which was right in his own eyes." It is clear that the author did not regard this as a good thing but as a disaster calling for dramatic and radical reform. Put it another way— there was no law in Israel because there was no prophet to interpret or king to enforce it. There were only "Judges", a term which to us is distinctly misleading; for the word translated "Judge" (Shophat) means not only to judge but to vindicate or deliver or simply to govern. The title therefore does not just describe the role of the leader as Judge so much as to designate a particular period in Israel's history when they were governed by chieftains rather than by kings. The literature on this subject is very large. (For a convenient summary see Moore in his ICC commentary on Judges.) It could be said that in the minds of those responsible for the final arrangement of the Old Testament documents, the Book of Judges is intended to show just how important it was that a monarchy should be founded which would be capable of guarding and ensuring obedience to the law of God. In your own mind abolish the Book of Ruth for a moment and read straight on from Judges 21, 25—"in those days there was no king in Israel and every man did what was right in his own eyes" to I Samuel 1, the story of Elkanah and Hannah. The connection between the two books is very close, for Samuel provides in his own person precisely what the period of the Judges lacked—a prophet capable of interpreting the law of God and a ruler capable of enforcing it. Samuel began as a little server at the altar; he grew into a formidable leader of men and an implacable enthusiast for the law.

Samuel acted as a judge in Israel as long as he lived
and every year went on circuit to Bethel and Gilgal

and Mizpah; he dispensed justice at all these places
returning always to Ramah. That was his home
and the place from which he governed Israel and
there he built an altar to the Lord. (I
Samuel 7: 15-17)

Just as Moses was a bridge between the enslavement in
Egypt and the invasion of Canaan, so Samuel is the bridge
figure between one transitory form of government (the
Judges) and the more permanent and infinitely more significant form of government (the Kings).

Samuel was a formidable personage for all the beguiling
circumstances which surrounded his birth and upbringing,
but his importance derives not so much from his personal
qualities or indeed his personal achievements as from the
crucial role he played in the history and theology of Israel. In
common with similar narratives elsewhere in Holy Scripture
his birth is seen as the "miraculous" response to the plea of a
barren woman and his upbringing is invested with supernatural significance. He is vowed to the Lord, he is dedicated
to the temple, he ministers before the Lord, he hears the voice
of God.

The Lord came and stood there, and called,
"Samuel, Samuel", as before. Samuel answered,
"Speak; thy servant hears thee." The Lord said,
"Soon I shall do something in Israel which will
ring in the ears of all who hear it. When that day
comes I will make good every word I have spoken
against Eli and his family from beginning to end.
You are to tell him that my judgment on his house
shall stand for ever because he knew of his sons'
blasphemies against God and did not rebuke them.
Therefore I have sworn to the family of Eli that
their abuse of sacrifices and offerings shall never be
expiated."
Samuel lay down till morning and then opened
the doors of the house of the Lord, but he was
afraid to tell Eli about the vision. Eli called Samuel:
"Samuel, my son," he said; and he answered,
"Here I am." Eli asked, "What did the Lord say to

you? Do not hide it from me. God forgive you if you hide one word of all that he said to you." Then Samuel told him everything and hid nothing. Eli said, "The Lord must do what is good in his eyes."

As Samuel grew up, the Lord was with him, and none of his words went unfulfilled. From Dan to Beersheba, all Israel recognized that Samuel was confirmed as a prophet of the Lord. So the Lord continued to appear in Shiloh, because he had revealed himself there to Samuel. (1 Sam. 3: 10-21)

He is clearly and unmistakably a prophet of the Lord raised up to perform a particular task—and that task is the creating of a monarchy which will be the guardian and exponent of the law of God. Not for nothing had Samuel ministered before the Ark of God in Shiloh containing the two tablets of stone.

The importance of the founding of the monarchy is illustrated not only by the detailed reminiscences of the birth and upbringing of Samuel, but by the space devoted to the earlier monarchy as distinct from the later. Recite the names of the Kings of Judah. Yes indeed, there were twenty-three of them plus or minus. And of Israel twenty-one. Yet in the Books recording their exploits, the first three kings, viz. Saul, David and Solomon between them command seventy-seven pages out of a total of 198. Or put it another way, 120 years of history are covered in seventy-seven pages; the rest (364 years) are covered in 121 pages. Arithmetic is not my strong point and careful readers may arrive at figures marginally different—but not much different. The message is that it is the founding of the monarchy and the significance of it which has captured the interest of the authors, not its history.

Now therefore we look at the origins of the monarchy. There are two narratives, so it is believed, of the anointing of Saul which lie rather uneasily side by side in the text. You can check it without difficulty by comparing e.g. I Samuel 8: 4-22 and I Samuel 9: 1-16. In the one the appointment arises out of the political situation described in I Samuel 8: 1-7.

When Samuel grew old, he appointed his sons to be

judges in Israel. The eldest son was named Joel and the second Abiah; they acted as judges in Beersheba. His sons did not follow in their father's footsteps but were intent on their own profit, taking bribes and perverting the course of justice. So all the elders of Israel met, and came to Samuel at Ramah and said to him, "You are now old and your sons do not follow in your footsteps; appoint us a king to govern us, like other nations." But their request for a king to govern them displeased Samuel and he prayed to the Lord. The Lord answered Samuel, "Listen to the people and all that they are saying; they have not rejected you, it is I whom they have rejected, I whom they will not have to be their king."

In that narrative the request for a monarchy is a challenge to the monarchy of God and is therefore to be regretted. In the other, Saul is sent to search out the lost asses and finds instead a kingdom (a typical example of Hebrew humour at its best) and his appointment is expressly commanded by God.

Now the day before Saul came, the Lord had disclosed his intention to Samuel in these words: "At this same time tomorrow I will send you a man from the land of Benjamin. Anoint him prince over my people Israel, and then he shall deliver my people from the Philistines. I have seen the sufferings of my people and their cry has reached my ears." The moment Saul appeared the Lord said to Samuel, "Here is the man of whom I spoke to you. This man shall rule my people." Saul came up to Samuel in the gateway and said, "Would you tell me where the seer lives?" Samuel replied, "I am the seer. Go on ahead of me to the hill-shrine and you shall eat with me today; in the morning I will set you on your way, after telling you what you have on your mind. Trouble yourself no more about the asses lost three days ago, for they have been found. But what is it that all Israel is

wanting? It is you and your ancestral house." "But
I am a Benjamite," said Saul, "from the smallest of
the tribes of Israel, and my family is the least
important of all the families of the tribe of Benjamin. Why do you say this to me?" Samuel then
brought Saul and his servant into the dining-hall
and gave them a place at the head of the company,
which numbered about thirty. Then he said to the
cook, "Bring the portion that I gave you and told
you to put on one side." So the cook took up the
whole haunch and leg and put it before Saul; and
Samuel said, "Here is the portion of meat kept for
you. Eat it: it has been reserved for you at this feast
to which I have invited the people." So Saul dined
with Samuel that day, and when they came down
from the hill-shrine to the city a bed was spread on
the roof for Saul, and he stayed there that night. At
dawn Samuel called to Saul on the roof, "Get up,
and I will set you on your way." When Saul rose,
he and Samuel went out together into the street. As
they came to the end of the town, Samuel said to
Saul, "Tell the boy to go on." He did so and then
Samuel said, "Stay here a moment, and I will tell
you the word of God." Samuel took a flask of oil
and poured it over Saul's head, and he kissed him
and said, "The Lord anoints you prince over his
people Israel; you shall rule the people of the Lord
and deliver them from the enemies round about
them. You shall have a sign that the Lord has
anointed you prince to govern his inheritance." (I
Sam. 9: 15—10: 1)

In passing, I draw your attention to the fact that in this
narrative the new ruler of Israel is described as prince or
leader not as king—which may or may not be significant, but
the intention is clear that the future King of Israel is
appointed as a result of a series of providential events
culminating in a meeting with Samuel who was forewarned
by God himself and responded in obedience to him.

Now what is the significance of these narratives of the
origins of the monarchy? The two accounts could be said to

represent two views of the monarchy nearly always at variance with each other in the actual history of the monarchy. To one school of thought the monarchy itself was a mistake forced upon a reluctant prophet in order that Israel should be "like the other nations" rather than different from the other nations, i.e. a peculiar people under the direct rule of God and the prophets as his representatives on earth. To the other school of thought the monarchy was the divinely given and authenticated means by which the anarchy of the Judges period was to be overcome and order was to be established under the law with the king as its guardian. This latter view is reflected in a notoriously difficult verse I Samuel 10: 25—"then Samuel told the people the manner of the kingdom and wrote it in a book and laid it up before the Lord" (AV). The word for "manner" is *mishpat* (derived from the same route as the word to judge)—which has a variety of meanings in the Old Testament of which ordinance or law is certainly one. We could be in the presence therefore of a striking example of the close association between the founding of the monarchy and the institution of a law relating to it. (See Edward Robertson—*The Old Testament Problem,* published by Manchester University Press, 1950.)

Whatever that verse may have meant to its author, or to the compiler responsible for the whole work, it could hardly have meant less than an appreciation of the connection in the author's or the compiler's mind between the monarchy, the law and the prophet. All three are represented in the verse. This may go some way to explain why Joshua-Judges-Samuel-Kings were called the "former prophets". They represent a prophetic view of the calling of Israel and of the authority behind the great institutions that constituted the nation. The king, whether by divine initiative or merely by divine inadvertence, is there to represent, in his own person, and in his activity, the law of God. He is subject to that law himself and woe betide the man, whether he be a David or an Ahab, who assumes autocratic powers and overrides the law in his own interests. The child born of the adulterous union between David and Bathsheba dies. The vineyard which Ahab coveted was to be the source of his own and his family's destruction. I recall, with some embarrassment now, my attempt at an exposition of the following passage for the benefit of the local Mothers' Union. It describes in matchless prose the death of Ahab's wife.

> Jehu came to Jezreel. Now Jezebel had heard what had happened; she had painted her eyes and dressed her hair, and she stood looking down from a window. As Jehu entered the gate, she said, "Is it peace, you Zimri, you murderer of your master?" He looked up at the window and said, "Who is on my side, who?" Two or three eunuchs looked out, and he said, "Throw her down." They threw her down, and some of her blood splashed on to the wall and the horses, which trampled her underfoot. Then he went in and ate and drank. "See to this accursed woman," he said, "and bury her; for she is a king's daughter." But when they went to bury her they found nothing of her but the skull, the feet, and the palms of the hands; and they went back and told him. Jehu said, "It is the word of the Lord which his servant Elijah the Tishbite spoke, when he said, 'In the plot of ground at Jezreel the dogs shall devour the flesh of Jezebel, and Jezebel's corpse shall lie like dung upon the ground in the plot at Jezreel so that no one will be able to say: This is Jezebel.' " (2 Kings 9: 30-37)

So perish all those, the writer is saying, who rely on kingly power to infringe the rights of their subjects contrary to the statutes and ordinances of Israel. "Thou shalt not bear false witness ... Thou shalt not steal ... Thou shalt do no murder ... Thou shalt not covet." At the throne of the lawgiver the law-breaker stands condemned. It is a mark of a high civilisation indeed even if devoid of the internal combustion engine and heavier-than-air flight, when the chief executive retains authority only in submitting himself to the authority of the law. But it was not only a question of personal conduct; the king was the minister of the law and it was precisely at this point that Absalom was able to alienate the affections of Israel to himself.

After this, Absalom provided himself with a chariot

and horses and an escort of fifty men. He made it a practice to rise early and stand beside the road which runs through the city gate. He would hail every man who had a case to bring before the king for judgment and would ask him what city he came from. When he answered, "I come, sir, from such and such a tribe of Israel," Absalom would say to him, "I can see that you have a very good case, but you will get no hearing from the king." And he would add, "If only I were appointed judge in the land, it would be my business to see that everyone who brought a suit or a claim got justice from me." Whenever a man approached to prostrate himself, Absalom would stretch out his hand, take hold of him and kiss him. By behaving like this to every Israelite who sought the king's justice, Absalom stole the affections of the Israelites. (II Sam. 15: 1-6)

Indolence and luxury had sapped the good king's energy and he had a rebellion on his hands.

Exemplar of the law in his personal life, minister of the law in his public life, the king was also the one responsible for imposing the law on a rebellious and gainsaying people. There are two dramatic examples of this in the former prophets. The first relates to the law-enforcing zeal of Hezekiah.

In the third year of Hoshea son of Elah king of Israel, Hezekiah son of Ahaz king of Judah became king. He was twenty-five years old when he came to the throne, and he reigned in Jerusalem for twenty-nine years; his mother was Abi daughter of Zechariah. He did what was right in the eyes of the Lord, as David his forefather had done. It was he who suppressed the hill-shrines, smashed the sacred pillars, cut down every sacred pole and broke up the bronze serpent that Moses had made; for up to that time the Israelites had been burning sacrifices to it; they called it Nehushtan. He put his trust in the Lord the God of Israel; there was nobody like him among all the kings of Judah who succeeded him or among those who had gone before him. He remained loyal to the Lord and did not fail in his allegiance to him, and he kept the commandments which the Lord had given to Moses. So the Lord was with him and he prospered in all that he undertook. (II Kings 18: 1-7)

It is said of Hezekiah that "he slept with his fathers", a blessing uncommon enough in the ancient world to be remarked upon. The second example is the story of Josiah.

And Hilkiah the high priest said to Shaphan the secretary, "I have found the book of the law in the house of the Lord." And Hilkiah gave the book to Shaphan, and he read it. And Shaphan the secretary came to the king, and reported to the king, "Your servants have emptied out the money that was found in the house, and have delivered it into the hand of the workmen who have the oversight of the house of the Lord." Then Shaphan the secretary told the king, "Hilkiah the priest has given me a book." And Shaphan read it before the king.

And when the king heard the words of the book of the law, he rent his clothes. And the king commanded Hilkiah the priest, and Ahikam the son of Shaphan, and Achbor the son of Micaiah, and Shaphan the secretary, and Asaiah the king's servant, saying, "Go, inquire of the Lord for me, and for the people, and for all Judah, concerning the words of this book that has been found; for great is the wrath of the Lord that is kindled against us, because our fathers have not obeyed the words of this book, to do according to all that is written concerning us."

Then the king sent, and all the elders of Judah and Jerusalem were gathered to him. And the king went up to the house of the Lord, and with him all the men of Judah and all the inhabitants of Jerusalem, and the priests and the prophets, all the people, both small and great; and he read in their hearing all the words of the book of the covenant which had been found in the house of the Lord. And the king stood by the pillar and made a covenant before the Lord, to walk after the Lord and to keep his commandments and his testimonies and his statutes, with all his heart and all his soul, to perform the words of this covenant that were written in this book; and all the people joined in the covenant. (II Kings 22: 8—23: 3, RSV)

Scholarly opinion is greatly divided, as it is always likely to be, about which book it was or what section of a book it was that was discovered, but the king was sufficiently impressed by its antiquity and evident authority to set in hand a drastic reform in the life of the nation. It is somewhat of an embarrassment to the author of this particular section of the former prophets that the good King Josiah for all his reforming zeal came to an unfortunate end. He was foolish enough to tangle with the King of Egypt and this laconic report marks the end of him.

In his days Pharaoh Neco king of Egypt went up to the king of Assyria to the river Euphrates. King Josiah went up to meet him; and Pharaoh Neco slew him at Megiddo, when he saw him. (II Kings 23: 29, RSV)

The former prophets cover the whole of the monarchical period from the origins of the monarchy until its demise, which the last chapter records in the following words:

In the ninth year of his reign, in the tenth month, on the tenth day of the month, Nebuchadnezzar king of Babylon advanced with all his army against Jerusalem, invested it and erected watch-towers against it on every side; the siege lasted till the eleventh year of King Zedekiah. In the fourth month of that year, on the ninth day of the month, when famine was severe in the city and there was no food for the common people, the city was thrown open. When Zedekiah king of Judah saw this, he and all his armed escort left the city and fled by night through the gate called Between the Two Walls, near the king's garden. They escaped towards the Arabah, although the Chaldaeans were surrounding the city. But the Chaldaean army pursued the king and overtook him in the lowlands of Jericho; and all his company was dispersed. The king was seized and brought before the king of Babylon at Riblah, where he pleaded his case before him. Zedekiah's sons were slain before his eyes; then his eyes were put out, and he was brought to Babylon in fetters of bronze. (II Kings 25: 1-7)

It would be difficult to exaggerate the traumatic effect of this event upon the life of Israel. Not only were they defeated, not only was their capital city destroyed and the temple with it, not only were they in exile, but the Davidic line created by God, authenticated by prophecy was gone forever. Never again could a son of David sit on the throne of Israel. That very institution which had guaranteed their relationship with God had been removed. The "former prophets" are in a sense a considered theological reflection upon that unspeakable event. The historian was saying with hindsight what for centuries the prophets had been saying with foresight. The prophets had threatened, cajoled, resisted the kings of Israel in an attempt to make them conform to the law of God of which they were the guardians. It was their failure to do so, the historian now says, which overturned God's purposes for them and issued in destruction for them and for their people. The prophet and the prophetic historian are at one. But while that may be true it is of scant comfort to the elect people of God who now languish in exile. So the prophetic historian throws out a lifeline in a desolate ocean. The monarchy, he says, was indeed of divine origin. One account of it, as we have seen, emphasises the rather grudging permission of God; the other offers a rather more encouraging picture. But both are one in the mind of the compiler who recalls his readers to the truth that God is the real king of Israel who for a time, willingly or unwillingly, delegated His authority to an earthly king, but remained Himself king even when the earthly king vanishes from the scene. A king is dead, long live the King. There is another sense in which the prophetic historian and the prophet are at one. The Davidic monarchy made deep ruts in the minds of the Davidic people. No visitor to Israel today can ever doubt that. David was not simply a person, however well favoured; he was a symbol, a symbol of a kingdom universal in extent founded upon divine law, animated by divine grace which would one day triumph over the mighty kingdoms of Egypt and Babylon and Rome and Peking and Moscow and Washington. In that sense, if in this sense alone, there was an incipient messianism both in the prophets and in the prophetic historians. They had lost a kingdom on earth, they would receive a kingdom from heaven, when the law would not be just inscribed on tablets of stone but on the hearts and minds of men. The would-be social reformer may not be eager to take this on board but he may find it is on board already. Twentieth-century civilisation may be closer than we imagine to sixth-century Israel and we could well profit from the reflections of the prophet and the prophetic historian as they viewed the perils of their people.

"Look," said God, "I wanted you the way you are and no different. You were a wanderer in my name and wherever you went you brought the settled folk a little homesickness for freedom."

Hesse
Knulp

V

Sinai

I can well imagine that the reader may be reacting to this excursus so far in one of two ways. If he is unfamiliar with the history of biblical studies over the past three centuries he may be wondering why I have taken so long to "prove" what he has always regarded as self-evident. He has always assumed that Israel had a law which was given to them at Sinai and to which kings and prophets subsequently appealed in their attempts to order the life of their people. To such a reader I can only say that he cannot be content with such an assumption insofar as it has been seriously challenged by generations of honest and learned scholars. If such a reader stands for the "Law of God" and is affronted or perplexed by other people's seeming indifference to it, it is not necessarily because "other people" are perverse; it could be that they simply do not share his assumptions. He and they are not speaking the same language; an abyss of incomprehension lies between them. It is important therefore that he who believes in the Law of God should become aware of the intellectual difficulties that attend to his belief and learn to qualify his certainty with a proper diffidence. Things are never quite so obvious as they seem and an appearance of dogmatic assurance can be counter-productive in terms of credibility and influence. If we are to persuade people that the Law of God, properly understood, is the way of blessedness and peace, we need, however superficially, to have passed through the academic mill, to sit where the critics sit, to face the facts in all their inconclusiveness. As a one-time teacher of the Old Testament, I had in the process to challenge and sometimes destroy the easy assumptions with which students came to their task. It was important not only for the sake of intellectual honesty but for the sake of a man's continuing ministry of the word. If he were to be genuinely rather than spuriously confident in the word he proclaimed, he needed to feel and to survive the icy draught of documentary and historical criticism. "Argument weak; shout louder," the old preacher used to write against the less convincing passages of his sermon. Dogmatic utterance can often shield a mind which has been untested by facts and, without altogether recognising it, is uncertain of them. "My mind is made up; don't confuse me with facts" is a common enough experience in many fields of human endeavour, and we continue to pay the price for this dogmatism both in social and personal terms. The would-be champion of the law of God needs to win his spurs before he can effectively confront the forces of disorder and anarchy in the world. For such a reader, therefore, these early chapters are intended as an elementary introduction to the complexities which arise from any set of ancient documents and not least from what the Jews and the Christians call the sacred Scriptures. I have been trying to put foundations under some common assumptions in order that they may not remain simply "assumptions" but may be based on a hard core of fact.

The other reader might react in the opposite way. He may be familiar with the arguments and counter-arguments of a thousand scholarly works and so far, although perhaps it is too much to hope, he will be with me all the way. Yes indeed, he believes that the Israelite monarchy arose out of the experience of chronic disorder in the Judges period and that the monarch was specifically made responsible for the inter-pretation and enforcement of the law. He believes also that the prophets were not just free agents of the spirit, spinning their oracles out of the air, but radical interpreters of the law who sought to regulate Israel's life on the basis of the law. He would agree that the evidence of the prophetic canon, all the more powerful for being indirect, is that Israel's national life was conducted on this basis. But two questions will arise in his mind. They are:

1.   What evidence is there that this law had a specific origin in the Wilderness period as the second canon of scripture suggests? May it not be that law arose out of the social/religious confusions of the early settlement in Canaan, was refined and codified in the Samuel period, and thus became the moral basis of Israel's life to which

kings and prophets legitimately appealed. This would not necessarily be to dispute the divine origin of the law, but to give it a different history from that which appears in the Books of Moses. But it would have the effect, nevertheless, of "locating" the law and seeing it as a distinct product of a distinct period in the life of a distinct people—without any necessary relevance to nations which do not happen to have grown up that way. Viewed in that light, the law of Israel is the law of Israel, no more, with no particular claim on us beyond the reverence we rightly give to antiquity and to age-old wisdom. This, therefore, is an important question which a well informed reader may well wish to address to me.

2. If we were able to dispose of the first question in a reasonably convincing way we would still be left with a second question and it is this—given that the Hebrews entered the Promised Land with a law given to them in the wilderness, have we any means of knowing precisely what that law was? After all, the references to the law in the prophetic canon are scattered and fugitive and we cannot be sure what part, if any, of the laws contained in the Pentateuch were accessible to the kings and prophets of the monarchical period. No scholar, Jewish or Christian, would dispute that the law as we have it now is the product of a long period of growth and adaptation. What stage had it reached when Joshua swept in with his triumphant troops to Canaan? Or, to put it another way, at what point in the growth of a tree do we say— "this is the trunk and these are the branches"? Or to put it yet another way "this is original; this is derived"? If we may revert to the historical imagery of the Scriptures, we are asking—what was on the tablets of stone to which kings and prophets appealed? This again is an important question and on the answer will depend our attitude towards law in general and to the law of the Hebrews in particular. The argument of this book will be that there are certain fundamental (or original) laws which no civilisation can afford to ignore and that these laws were "revealed" at a particular point in the history of a particular people at a particular place. The argument, of

course, is incapable of being proved, but I shall hope in this chapter and the one that follows it, to offer reasons why we at least have to take the proposition seriously. The mere act of taking the argument seriously may lead us to take the whole principle of law more seriously. Law is too important a matter to be left either to lawyers or to textual critics.

The reader who comes to the serious study of the Bible for the first time will need to know that the Pentateuch is a composite book. It could hardly be otherwise with a series of documents covering centuries of history and containing many separate and sometimes divergent traditions. I will not burden you with a discussion of how these traditions relate to each other, because the details can be found in any introduction to the Old Testament. What is perhaps not so obvious, is that these varying traditions were at a stage in their development subsumed under a literary whole which has its own momentum and its own rationale. It is refreshing to find this emphasis recovered in the recent commentary on Exodus by Dr. Brevard Childs who in his introduction says:

> From a literary point of view there is a great need
> to understand the present composition as a piece of
> literature with its own integrity. The concentration
> of critical scholars on form-critical and source
> analysis has tended to fragment the text and leave
> the reader with only bits and pieces. (*Exodus*—
> Brevard Childs, SCM Press)

Of even more importance, as Dr. Childs suggests later, is the fact that the literary format is itself subject to a consistent theological view of Israel's origin and of her role in the purpose of God. The book which we have before us deserves to be treated as a whole. There was a moment in time when, to put it our way, the book rolled off the presses entitled "The Books of Moses", and we are free to presume that those responsible for its final shape not only handled the literary material at their disposal but had a theological point to make.

Treated as a literary whole, the Pentateuch centres down on the event which is here described.

On the third day, when morning came, there were peals of thunder and flashes of lightning, dense cloud on the mountain and a loud trumpet blast; the people in the camp were all terrified.
Moses brought the people out from the camp to meet God, and they took their stand at the foot of the mountain. Mount Sinai was all smoking because the Lord had come down upon it in fire; the smoke went up like the smoke of a kiln; all the people were terrified, and the sound of the trumpet grew even louder. Whenever Moses spoke, God answered him in a peal of thunder. (Exodus 19: 16-19)

Then follows the recital of the Ten Commandments in the form more or less familiar to us and then:

When all the people saw how it thundered and the lightning flashed, when they heard the trumpet sound and saw the mountain smoking, they trembled and stood at a distance. "Speak to us yourself," they said to Moses, "and we will listen; but if God speaks to us we shall die." Moses answered, "Do not be afraid. God has come only to test you, so that the fear of him may remain with you and keep you from sin." So the people stood at a distance, while Moses approached the dark cloud where God was. (Exodus 20: 18-21)

Even when protected by the cool literary English of the New English Bible we are in the presence of what is clearly a stupendous spiritual experience. We have no means of assessing the accuracy of the narrative or of rationalising the phenomena associated with it. It is just there. It needs perhaps to be said that profound spiritual experiences recorded in the Bible, of which this is one, are not recorded just for their own sake. Their importance resides in the fact that they accompany moments of supreme significance in the life of the chosen people. They are seen to authenticate certain characteristic religious institutions. So, for example, the word from heaven which came to Abraham on Mount

Moriah, where he was about to sacrifice his son, Isaac, would be associated in the mind, both of the writer and of the reader, with the sacrificial system of Israel which replaced the child sacrifices of the surrounding nations. Similarly, when the spirit came upon the Elders of Israel in the wilderness (Numbers 11: 25), the incident would be seen as the origin of that authoritative body in Israel, which later came to be known as the Sanhedrin. So, in the case we are now considering, the phenomena of smoke and fire and the voice from Heaven, serve to enthrone the law which was given at Sinai, as supreme in the life of the people; it is the very voice of God to them, rendered unmistakable by the visible and audible splendours which surrounded the Mount. We may judge that the people of Israel at that point were confronted with one of the not infrequent volcanic eruptions associated with the Sinai range. If it indeed was so, it would not have affected the writer's judgment on the matter; natural phenomena and historical events were alike to him a means of revelation.

We have no access to the Sinai of 3,500 years ago. There is no fire or cloud to be seen and no voice to be heard now. But this would have been no problem to the author, even allowing for the fact that he may have been writing centuries after the event. For him it is not just that the event authenticated the law; it is that the existence of the law inscribed on stone and embedded in the hearts of his people testifies to the event. It would be his conviction that he is describing the most important event in the history of the world and he would not be surprised that it should be accompanied by the visible and audible signs of God's presence. It would have struck him as odd if he had been asked to believe that Moses had jotted down the Ten Commandments in a moment's reverie over his morning coffee. I have put it in that extravagant way to emphasise how vast is the gulf between the author's mental and spiritual scenery and our own and to suggest, incidentally, that our way of interpreting events is not the only way.

"The most important event in the history of the world." Is there any way that such a claim can be justified? It is important to realise that the division of the Pentateuch into the five books is unlikely to be original. It is a mistake, therefore, to switch off at the end of Genesis and to switch on again at the beginning of Exodus. Remove the artificial chapter barrier and the structure of the whole book becomes clearer. The Book of Genesis describes a world marred by disorder. Adam and Eve, so tradition goes, enjoyed the blessings of Paradise; they did not need fire and smoke to remind them of the presence of God. They walked with him in the cool of the evening and heard his voice like a whisper on the breeze. But they resisted the will of God and a whole chain of events followed from this action. Cain rose up and murdered his brother. The earth was filled with violence and men made instruments of war. The story of the Tower of Babel is a simple testimony to the fact that men were scattered over the face of the earth and ceased to be able to communicate with each other. Sodom and Gomorrah go up in smoke with the lawlessness of those two cities of the plain. The scenario is familiar enough; it could have been written by a twentieth-century historian as easily as by a Hebrew theologian of three thousand years ago. We respond to violence on the earth with international action and schemes of relief, with conferences and peace-keeping forces. The Hebrew responded with a trenchant comment on the human condition—"the imagination of man's heart is evil from his youth" (Genesis 8: 21, RSV) and with a provisional remedy for it (give him his due—it was only provisional). He saw the giving of the law at Sinai as God's response to men's need, offering him a way to "Paradise" where men would live at peace with each other, where swords would be beaten into plough shares and the lion would lie down with the lamb. The law delivered into the hand of Moses was to be the way of blessedness and peace, first of all for the chosen people, but then for all mankind, on whose behalf the chosen people had been chosen. There is little doubt in my own mind that this is a legitimate way of interpreting the documents we have in front of us and indeed I presume to believe that it is the only way. It is certainly the way in which the prophets and the prophetic writers of the second canon themselves interpreted it. In the wilderness of Sinai God had taken his child Israel by the hand and had taught him how to walk.

In between the description of the chaotic condition of mankind in the prehistoric period and the giving of the law at Sinai, is the event which marked off Israel as the chosen people, chosen to be the agents of God and instruments of God's law. The first figure in the Bible who could be regarded as, in one sense or another, "historical" is Abraham. We may see him through a glass darkly, but modern scholarship is more disposed than it used to be to see that he was there. Patriarchal narratives do not seek simply to associate the Hebrew people with Abraham, Isaac and Jacob, but to explain what was an inexpugnable part of the Hebrew's racial memory, viz. the bondage in Egypt. I myself, would believe this to be, if anything could ever be, part of sober history, despite all the arguments that have been raised against it. No one invents a slave background. Israel's persistent hostility to Egypt, everywhere reflected in her literature, was not just due to the depredations of a stronger military power. Israel in fact suffered infinitely more from the Empires of Assyria and Babylon than she did from Egypt. But they could never expunge from their minds the memories of the "house of bondage". They had been slaves and could never forget it. So the Book of Genesis describes how it came to be—a famine in Canaan, a Hebrew immigrant (Joseph) in a position of authority in Pharaoh's court, the subsequent settlement in Goshen, the rise of a regime hostile to foreigners—and then the taskmasters and the whip, and the subsistence living and the attempted genocide. Moses was raised up to deliver his people and they came out of Egypt by the mighty hand of God with all the odds stacked against them. But to the Hebrew theologian it was not just another liberation movement or a "long march". They were delivered from one unwanted bondage in order to subject themselves to another. The route from Egypt led infallibly to Sinai, from the law of Egypt to the law of God. And the object of that long drawn out tribal history, stemming from Abraham as much as four hundred years before, was the giving of the law to the people chosen to receive it on behalf of all mankind on whose behalf Israel had been chosen. It is a view of history, which at first sight seems unbelievably narrow, but on reflection unbelievably broad; for it takes into its compass the emergence of man on the face of the earth, his painful struggles for identity and relationship, his search for truth and order, and sees it as a journey from savagery to civilisation, from chaos to cosmos, from Eden to Paradise.

Give the author his due, he is a man of far horizons who yet perceives that the problems of God are exercised in and through the sensitivity and obedience of individual men (Abraham, Joseph, Moses) and in the corporate obedience of societies (Israel) to the law which was revealed. Nowhere in the history of mankind is so much seen to depend on so few.

Everything before Sinai leads up to it, everything after Sinai leads from it, it is the central point of Israel's history and the most important event in the history of the world. So we are asked to believe. Between Sinai, however, and the events described in Samuel, Kings and the prophets another institution emerges which would be wholly familiar to those for whom the authors wrote. The temple which Solomon built after the settlement in Canaan was the joy of all the earth and singularly impressive. But it had modest beginnings. It began with a box elaborately decorated no doubt, but a box—in which were kept two tablets of stone. This box was sometimes carried in battle, was lost to the Philistines for a period of time, and was eventually housed in the temple which was built for it at Jerusalem. There it became the centre of the cult and was housed in the holiest place of all into which the High Priest entered once a year. You will hardly need to be told there is a huge literature around the history of the Ark, so-called, and many a theory about how it looked and what it meant. But there is a tradition firmly built into the life and literature of Israel that this box contained amongst other things two tablets of stone bearing the ten words of God. It is a strange thought that the imageless worship of Almighty God should be for ever associated in the Hebrew mind with two tablets of stone containing the ten words. Priests abased themselves before it, singers sang around it, incense was burned, prophecies were uttered and Yahweh was enthroned above it, men died to protect it, enemies laboured exceedingly to destroy it. Perhaps they need not have bothered. It is lost forever, so tradition goes, in some mountain cave, hidden there, it is supposed, by Jeremiah before the Babylonians took the city. It was not needed any more; it had entrenched itself in the faith and worship of the chosen people and to this day in synagogues all over the world the worship of Israel takes place before the "Holy Ark" containing the Scrolls of the Law. The day would surely come when the words written on the tablets of stone will be written on the hearts of men for their blessing and their peace.

> " 'Return, O faithless children, says
> the Lord;
> for I am your master;
> I will take you, one from a city and
> two from a family,
> and I will bring you to Zion.
> " 'And I will give you shepherds after my own heart, who will feed you with knowledge and understanding. And when you have multiplied and increased in the land, in those days, says the Lord, they shall no more say, "The ark of the covenant of the Lord." It shall not come to mind, or be remembered, or missed; it shall not be made again. At that time Jerusalem shall be called the throne of the Lord, and all nations shall gather to it, to the presence of the Lord in Jerusalem, and they shall no more stubbornly follow their own evil heart.' "
> (Jer. 3: 14-17, RSV)

It is indeed a strange story; I am only half inclined to believe it. But if it is true in any sense whatsoever it has something to say to society which society needs to hear. For it would seem that civilisation (which depends in large measure upon the rule of law) calls for the patient explication of, and costly obedience to, the law of God once written on tablets of stone at Sinai. The history of Israel is the history par excellence of the establishment of the law of God as a principle of life imperfectly understood indeed in Israel, and only half-heartedly obeyed but nevertheless held in trust for all mankind. The cloud over Sinai was pregnant with consequences which went far beyond the destiny of that little Middle-Eastern tribe and will effect us all to the end of time. We may choose to turn aside from Sinai to seek our promised land by a less arduous route but it is still there, brooding over the desert we have made for ourselves—and we may have to retrace our steps to it and hear again the Word of God amidst the fire and the smoke.

He wore the heavy tablets
Next to his skin,
They were his clothes, his burden
And his home,
Still within
He bore the distant voice
Of thunder,
Distillation of the word,
And he obeyed, and lived
Lived, and obeyed
The Law was freedom
Freedom was the Law.

from *Son of Abraham*
Susan Williams

VI

Tablets of Stone

We have reached the vantage point of Sinai and it is time to look back over the country we have so far traversed. The indirect, though I believe incontrovertible, evidence of the prophets is that they appealed to a body of law already in existence and largely familiar to, though often unobserved by, the people of Israel. It is no longer so confidently claimed as once it was that the prophets were effectively the creators of the ethico/religious institution we now call Judaism. They were not originators but radical interpreters of the law of God. The other half of the second canon, which we are accustomed to call the historical writings, likewise testifies to the role of the king as the upholder and administrator of the law already, in some form, received. Prophets and kings, therefore, though often at variance with each other, both appealed to a certain "deposit" of Torah which they supposed to have originated in the wilderness period. But the question any student is bound to ask is—were they right in appealing to the history of their people in this way? Is there sober evidence which can give credibility to the narratives of Genesis, Exodus and Numbers, with their message of the bondage in Egypt, the miraculous deliverance across the Red Sea and the para-normal experiences associated with the sacred mountain of Sinai? That is an important question for the argument of this book because on the answer depends our attitude to that body of literature in the Old Testament which we call the Torah of God. If it is no more than the casual outcrop of the civil and political life of an unimportant tribe then it is difficult to see how it can have any importance to those of us who live in a world so markedly different from the world of the second millennium before Christ. If, on the other hand, we see the Torah as the authentic Word of God given under highly exceptional circumstances at the end of a chain of historical events unique in the history of mankind, then we have to take seriously the possibility that the Torah, thus delivered, is intended to be of permanent significance for all mankind. I lose no opportunity of expressing and re-expressing the argument this way because it is of cardinal importance in forming our attitude to not just a form of words embedded in an ancient literature but to the Torah of God in general. Is there "One" who teaches mankind the way of truth—from the mountain of Sinai or from the lakeside of Galilee—or are we on our own in a wholly mysterious, historical process without path or light or compass or destination? The pursuit of the reality behind the ancient documents of the Old Testament and the scarcely less ancient documents of the New, is no academic exercise invented for the discomfiture of generations of theological students. It is strictly *ad rem.* What we do in the Courts, what policemen do on the beat, what we seek to achieve in the prisons, will unconsciously depend on what we make of the stupendous event traditionally associated with Sinai at about 1400 B.C.

The argument of the preceding chapter was that making every allowance for the accidents of oral tradition and written text, the Book of Exodus is substantially correct in its understanding of Israel's history. They were enslaved; they did escape; they did go to Sinai; Moses did receive a message from the One whom he supposed to be the God of Abraham, Isaac and Jacob; and that message is to be discovered within the pages of Holy Scripture as we now have it. I repeat, "the message is to be discovered". For all the dedicated and skilful scholarship that has been poured into the study of these ancient documents, we still have to say that the message is yet to be discovered. The Torah, even as represented within what Christians call the Old Testament, is a large and confusing body of material. It is not supposed by any scholar that it was all vouchsafed in a matter of hours to Moses on the mountain top, nor indeed that it was all inscribed on tablets of stone. If the Torah of God is to be of any significance to us we must have some means of distinguishing between the Word of God to Moses and that Word as it is elaborated and refined in Scripture and Targum. In short, we need to distinguish between the original and the derived. As an example of the difficulty implicit in this exercise I quote from Gordon

Jessup's useful outline of Jewish life and faith, *No Strange God*:

> Orthodox Jews today sometimes use the word "Torah" to describe the whole body of authoritative Jewish "Law", biblical and post-biblical. As the Oral Law developed over the centuries, so, necessarily, did Jewish belief and practice.
>
> After the production of the Mishnah, completed by Rabbi Judah the Prince in about A.D. 200, the process of analysis and detailed explanation continued—now expounding the Mishnah, as well as the Scriptures themselves. Over the next three hundred years this resulted in a further body of teaching known as the Gemara. Gemara and Mishnah together make up the Talmud. This comprises six thousand folio pages of laws, legal decisions, illustrative stories and legends, moral and religious teachings. It deals with everything from the grand rituals of high festivals in the Temple, to the smallest detail concerning what may be carried on the Sabbath (without being forbidden as a burden), or the degree to which a man is responsible for the goods he sells to another.

Edward Robertson in the chapter entitled "The Riddle of the Torah" in his book *The Old Testament Problem* carves through centuries of scholarly debate with his view of the proper distinction between the original and the derived:

> We need have no hesitation in deciding where to look for our nucleus of the Torah. Rabbinic tradition is insistent that the Ten Commandments, the Decalogue, formed the foundation on which the Torah rested. According to the Palestinian Talmud, Hananiah, nephew of R. Joshua, said that on the tables of the Law after each commandment the laws derived from it were engraved, and R. Simon b. Lakish introduced in this connection the simile of the sea with a few great waves and a large number of small waves interspersed. This conveys the idea,

early held and widely propagated in later Rabbinic circles, that the Ten Commandments served as rubrics for the rest of the 613 commandments of the Torah, which were summarised and arranged accordingly.

I myself accept this judgment but we need to recognise that it is far from being indisputable. And this is what many readers may find surprising if they have been brought up within the sound of the Ten Commandments as part of the Liturgy, or have attended churches where the Ten Commandments are engraved on the wall behind the altar, or have dim memories of the Catechism. Surely, they will say, there is something aboriginal, fixed, eternal about the Ten Commandments. It is part of the argument of this book that this is indeed so but it is not so obvious as we might suppose. Here again it is a matter of putting foundations under a too-ready assumption, of accounting for what we think we already know. The literature surrounding the history of the Ten Commandments is in fact enormous and exceedingly obscure, hidden away, as much of it is, in learned articles and footnotes. I can attempt only the most perfunctory treatment of the material available to us.

We need not, I think, be detained by the difficulties which present themselves in the sacred narrative itself. We have no means of knowing exactly what happened on the mountain (Moses was there alone), or what it means to say that the Ten Commandments were inscribed by the finger of God. But if we are to accept Edward Robertson's judgment previously quoted we have a right to ask what finally appeared on the two tablets of stone which, so it is alleged, found their way into the ark. If we seek to build civilisation anew on the revealed Torah of God we need to know what was on those stones, important as they were, and could be still in the history of mankind. It will be obvious to even a casual reader of the Old Testament that the two versions of the Commandments recorded in Exodus 20: 1-17 and in Deuteronomy 5: 6-21 are not identical. I take just one example regarding the Sabbath:

Remember to keep the sabbath day holy. You have

six days to labour and do all your work. But the
seventh day is a sabbath of the Lord your God; that
day you shall not do any work, you, your son or
your daughter, your slave or your slave-girl, your
cattle or the alien within your gates; for in six days
the Lord made heaven and earth, the sea, and all
that is in them, and on the seventh day he rested.
Therefore the Lord blessed the sabbath day and
declared it holy. (Exodus 20: 8-11)

Keep the sabbath day holy as the Lord your God
commanded you. You have six days to labour and
do all your work. But the seventh day is a sabbath
of the Lord your God; that day you shall not do any
work, neither you, your son or your daughter, your
slave or your slave-girl, your ox, your ass, or any of
your cattle, nor the alien within your gates, so that
your slaves and slave-girls may rest as you do.
Remember that you were slaves in Egypt and the
Lord your God brought you out with a strong hand
and an outstretched arm, and for that reason the
Lord your God commanded you to keep the
sabbath day." (Deut. 5: 12-15)

Sabbath observance was a highly distinctive feature of Israel's
life and one which marked them out amongst the nations of
the world. As you will see from the following quotations, the
Hebrew sabbath was often associated verbally at least with
the festival of the new moon, but that is not to say that they
were identical or that the one arose out of the other.

No more shall you trample my courts.
The offer of your gifts is useless,
the reek of sacrifice is abhorrent to me.
New moons and sabbaths and assemblies,
sacred seasons and ceremonies, I cannot endure.
(Isa. 1: 13)

"Why go to him today?" he asked. "It is neither
new moon nor sabbath." (II Kings 4: 23)

> When will the new moon be over so that we may
> sell corn? When will the sabbath be past so that we
> may open our wheat again, giving short measure in
> the bushel and taking overweight in the silver,
> tilting the scales fraudulently, and selling the dust
> of the wheat? (Amos 8: 5)

Whatever the sabbath originally meant, the author of
Exodus and the author of Deuteronomy part company on
what it meant respectively to them. In Exodus the sabbath is
attributed to the fact that God himself rested on the seventh
day from all his work; therefore we should do the same. In
Deuteronomy the sabbath is attributed to the experience of
the Exodus; it was because they were slaves in Egypt and
God brought them out with a strong hand and outstretched
arm. Thus in this author's mind the sabbath celebrated
Israel's national freedom from subjugation in Egypt. The two
explanations of the same religious practice are clearly
different though not of course exclusive of each other. This
seems to suggest two factors which we have always to bear in
mind in connection with the decalogue.

1. That it was the subject of continuous growth and
    development and was affected by the social and theologi-
    cal climate in which it was expounded. Thus the tenth
    Commandment in Deuteronomy gives priority to the
    neighbour's wife, whereas in Exodus priority is given to
    the neighbour's house. The process of explanation and
    application continues to this day in the practice of
    Judaism.

2. That the fact that there are differing explanations of the
    same practice testifies in itself to the belief that there was
    something to be explained. The sabbath was observed
    long before scholars began to find explanations for it, so
    a variety of explanations testifies to the existence of the
    sabbath rather than casts doubt upon it.

If, then, we allow for minor, and sometimes major,
alterations in the course of transmission can we be anything
like certain about their original form? Anthony Phillips in his

book *Ancient Israel's Criminal Law* argues that "all the Ten Commandments consisted of short apodictic injunctions which together make up what is now termed the Sinai Decalogue". This conclusion would no doubt have been supported by Edward Robertson in the light of his own comments in *The Old Testament Problem*:

> We have the Decalogue in two forms as given in Exodus 20: 2-17, and Deuteronomy 5: 6-21. That the "Ten Words" were given originally in shorter form is generally recognised by modern scholarship. It might be said that Jewish belief is disposed to support this, since there is a Rabbinic tradition, to which R. Haninah b. Gamaliel has given voice, that five commandments were written on each table, although according to other sages they were complete on each table. There was a further belief that the laws were so arranged as to correspond on the two tables. Thus the first law stood opposite to the sixth, the second opposite to the seventh, and so on. Only a visualisation of the commandments in shorter form would seem to make this possible. The original form of the Ten Words would be simple.

> Thou shalt have no other gods before me.
> Thou shalt not make unto thee a graven image.
> Thou shalt not take the name of the Lord, thy God, in vain.
> Remember the Sabbath day to keep it holy.
> Honour thy father and thy mother.
> Thou shalt not kill.
> Thou shalt not commit adultery.
> Thou shalt not steal.
> Thou shalt not bear false witness (against thy neighbour).
> Thou shalt not covet.

> That the additional matter which is found in the Decalogue has been added later is made the more probable by the fact that there is variation in respect of it in the two forms of the Decalogue. We

> could not expect to find differences in the shorter
> and basic form of the commandments, and there is
> none.

To say that "we could not expect to find differences in the
shorter and basic form of the commandments, and there is
none" is perhaps not wholly true because there is considerable diversity in the order in which the last five commandments are quoted outside the Books of Exodus and
Deuteronomy. In some variant texts of the Old Testament the
order is stealing, adultery, murder. In Philo it is adultery,
murder, stealing. In some versions of the Septuagint it is
adultery, stealing, murder. And in the ancient Christian
document, the so-called Didache, it is murder, adultery,
stealing, coveting, false witness. But, the order apart, I am
inclined to believe that we do have access to a form of words
which can be firmly associated with the experience of Sinai. It
is this form of words rather than any other which underlies
the massive development of Jewish law, and when isolated
from that massive development, could well be seen as the
original Torah of God intended for all mankind and not just
for Israel. We may therefore continue to respond with
confidence to the reading of the Ten Commandments in the
sacred Liturgy and, if we have a mind to, write them up
behind the altar. We may indeed appeal to them when
dealing with the disorders of our common life or deciding
whether we are permitted to commit adultery or not, or when
we pass judgment on a society as devoted as ours seems to be
to the "coveting" principle. Whether the argument so far is
right in detail or not, no scholar would dispute the antiquity
of these words and their importance in creating the
civilisation in which we live. Even if they were not the words
of God they are the words of ancient mankind to modern
mankind.

It would be easier for me, and probably for you, to stop just
there. But it is hardly legitimate to do so in view of the doubts
that surround not just the form of words but the precise
significance of those words. Some of us are long conditioned
to accept them as they are without observing the strangeness
of their association together. The first three commandments,
and the fourth (on any interpretation) exist together. They

describe an attitude to God, and the fifth commandment could be said to belong to the same category. I quote Anthony Phillips—"its concern was with relation with Jahwe for its aim was to secure that sons would automatically maintain the faith of their parents" (*Ancient Israel's Criminal Law*, page 81). If that is so we have two tablets of stone—the one relating to our duty to God and the other relating to our duty to our neighbour. So he who disputes the first table created, so he would say, out of a dubious hypothesis about the existence of God, may nevertheless freely assent to the second table which is primarily concerned with our neighbour, whose existence we cannot doubt. But even the second table is not without its perplexities. I shall have to refer the reader at this point to the detailed exegesis in Anthony Phillips' book which is, I think, the most recent substantial work in English on the subject. The argument of the book is that the Decalogue constitutes the basis of Israel's *criminal* law. But for all the skill and knowledge deployed the argument encounters obvious difficulties when applied to the tenth commandment. As Brevard Childs says in his commentary on Exodus (page 425)—"the verb used for 'covet' appears to denote a subjective emotion whereas all the preceding prohibitions were directed against an objective action." To put the issue more pointedly—how would an English J.P. handle a case in which the defendant was accused of coveting his neighbour's lawnmower or his neighbour's hi-fi apparatus or even his neighbour's wife. Brevard Childs draws I think the only conclusion that can be drawn—that "the original command was directed to that desire which included of course those intrigues which led to the acquiring of the coveted object." So Ahab began by coveting Naboth's vineyard but the coveting became explicit only in the intrigues and actions which led to the acquiring of Naboth's vineyard. The fact of the matter is that these commandments do not conform to any one category nor can they be interpreted in a uniform way. In that respect, if in that respect alone, they do not conform to what most of us understand by a law code. All the more reason therefore for believing that there is an element of orginality about them which defies rational explanation and refuses to be confined within the normal categories of thought. The Decalogue is not just "ancient

Israel's criminal law" or just a handbook of ethics or a guide to social conduct or the standards by which a believer may judge his attitudes. It is *sui generis*—a strange combination of precept and prohibition, of religion and ethics, of prohibited acts and prohibited intentions. It makes me doubtful whether Moses jotted them down in a moment of inner tension or that they arose by a process of trial and error out of the social and personal perplexities of the chosen people. There is a sense in which they are handed down complete, irrefrageable and wholly mysterious. They exist, awkward and challenging, like rocks that arise out of a smooth sea, guiding and at the same time impeding those who swim off that shore.

The reader will hardly need to be told that this author is not the first to have grappled ineffectively with the history and significance of these remarkable words which we call the Decalogue. If Justin Irenaeus and Tertullian, Augustine and Aquinas, Luther and Calvin, Barth and Tillich failed to resolve all the difficulties, who am I to succeed? I end however on a more positive note by asking you to attend to a series of reflections which ends Brevard Childs' section on the Decalogue.

1. The commandments are given by God as an expression of his will for his covenant people. They are not to be seen as simply moral directives apart from the living authority of God himself, who has made himself known.

2. The commandments are given by God to his people in the context of a covenant. Whatever broader implications the commandments may have, their primary function is directed toward shaping the life of his chosen community.

3. The commandments are addressed to the church both as a gracious gift pointing to the way of life and joy, and as a warning against sin which leads to death and judgment.

4. The intent of the commandments is to engender love of God and love of neighbor. These two sides cannot

be fused into one command, nor can either be used at the expense of the other. The church cannot love God apart from service to neighbor; however, there can be no true service of neighbor apart from the love of God.

5. The church strives to be obedient to the will of God through the gift of the Spirit of Christ, which continues to open up new and fresh avenues of freedom. This transformation of the law through Jesus Christ guards against both a deadening legalism and an uncharted enthusiasm in which the life of the church in and for the world is endangered.

The theological challenge for the church today is to give to the divine commandments a form of "flesh and blood" which not only strives to be obedient in the hearing of his word, but is equally serious in addressing its imperatives with boldness to the contemporary world. The church must speak to a thoroughly secular age which no longer understands the meaning of a divine word.

This is a model of judicious and sensitive comment in an area of unexampled confusion and debate. Observe the close association the author makes between the religious statement incorporated in the first four commandments and responsibility to the neighbour incorporated in the last five. Faith in God and respect for men are inextricably associated. Observe also the special role attributed to the commandments in the ordering of the life of the chosen community, which suggests what is indeed evident in Hebrew religion throughout, that duty to God carries with it responsibility for the corporate life of society. And finally observe that the commandments are to be seen not as a regrettable burden to be borne but as a "gracious gift pointing to the way of life and joy". Those words written on tablets of stone by the finger of God remain a challenge to the Church in its responsibility for a well-ordered society, and a challenge to society to take seriously what the Church believes it holds in trust for all mankind.

> Search into days gone by, long before your time, beginning at the day when God created man on earth; search from one end of heaven to the other, and ask if any deed as mighty as this has been seen or heard. Did any people ever hear the voice of God speaking out of the fire, as you heard it, and remain alive? Or did ever a god attempt to come and take a nation for himself away from another nation, with a challenge, and with signs, portents, and wars, with a strong hand and an outstretched arm, and with great deeds of terror, as the Lord your God did for you in Egypt in the sight of you all? You have had sure proof that the Lord is God; there is no other. From heaven he let you hear his voice for your instruction, and on earth he let you see his great fire, and out of the fire you heard his words. (Deut. 4: 32-36)

Yes, in my mind we have a sure proof—we hear the voice of God speaking out of the fire.

Man is free if he needs to obey no person but solely the laws.

Kant

We have but one prejudice. That is to uphold the law. And that we will do, whatever befall. Nothing shall deter us from doing our duty.

Lord Denning
Appeal Court, 27 January, 1977

VII

The Jews at Home

The argument so far has been that the documents, historical and prophetic, of the period of the monarchy, bear witness
to a body of law centred on the ten words to which both king
and prophet appealed. That law was part of an agreement or
"covenant" between Israel and Israel's God which was
intended to procure a society faithful in its worship of the one
God and just in the dealings of its members with each other.
Thus the whole nation was to walk in the way of blessedness
and peace. There are reasonable grounds for believing that
this law to which prophet and king appealed was the product
of the Wilderness period and emerged out of a series of
portentous events associated with a mountain in the Sinai
Peninsula.

The history of the founding of the kingdom, we have
already described in Chapter III. It is necessary only to
remember at this point that the united kingdom of Israel did
not long survive Solomon's death and thereafter we are
concerned with two kingdoms, the northern one with its
capital in Samaria, and the southern one with its capital in
Jerusalem. After a brief and turbulent history, Samaria fell to
the Assyrians in 721 B.C. Northern Israel was stripped of its
leading citizens and repopulated with men of mixed race—a
familiar stratagem in the ancient world intended to destroy
national identity and thus reduce the risk of rebellion. In
Samaria we shall have to say that this policy was wholly
successful. The ten tribes of Israel vanished without trace
underneath the dominant cultures of the surrounding nations.
Perhaps not entirely without trace, for the pilgrim to the
Holy Land may still encounter the remnants of a community
on Mount Gerizim and be shown poignant reminders of a
religious community which once flourished there in the first
millennium B.C. But of nationhood nothing remains except
the melancholy reminders of greatness which the pilgrim may

contemplate in the ruins of Tirzah and Samaria, of Megiddo and Hazor. But even those ruins are a reminder that of the two Israelite kingdoms the northern kingdom was, in terms of power, influence and population, infinitely greater than the southern. This is not altogether apparent in the Hebrew documents available to us, because those documents largely grew up under the influence of institutions in the southern kingdom and, therefore, tend to belittle the size and achievements of the northern kingdom. There was, of course, no love lost between them from the day when Jeroboam rebelled against the heir of David, Rehoboam, as that event is recorded in I Kings 12:

> Rehoboam went to Shechem, for all Israel had gone there to make him king. When Jeroboam son of Nebat, who was still in Egypt, heard of it, he remained there, having taken refuge there to escape King Solomon. They now recalled him, and he and all the assembly of Israel came to Rehoboam and said, "Your father laid a cruel yoke upon us; but if you will now lighten the cruel slavery he imposed on us and the heavy yoke he laid on us, we will serve you." "Give me three days," he said, "and come back again." So the people went away. King Rehoboam then consulted the elders who had been in attendance on his father Solomon while he lived: "What answer do you advise me to give to this people?" And they said, "If today you are willing to serve this people, show yourself their servant now and speak kindly to them, and they will be your servants ever after." But he rejected the advice which the elders gave him. He next consulted those who had grown up with him, the young men in attendance, and asked them, "What answer do you advise me to give to this people's request that I should lighten the yoke which my father laid on them?" The young men replied, "Give this answer to the people who say that your father made their yoke heavy and ask you to lighten it; tell them: 'My little finger is thicker than my father's loins. My father laid a heavy yoke on you; I will make it

heavier. My father used the whip on you; but I will
use the lash.' " Jeroboam and the people all came
back to Rehoboam on the third day, as the king had
ordered. And the king gave them a harsh answer.
He rejected the advice which the elders had given
him and spoke to the people as the young men had
advised: "My father made your yoke heavy; I will
make it heavier. My father used the whip on you;
but I will use the lash." So the king would not
listen to the people; for the Lord had given this turn
to the affair, in order that the word he had spoken
by Ahijah of Shiloh to Jeroboam son of Nebat
might be fulfilled.

When all Israel saw that the king would not
listen to them, they answered:

> What share have we in David?
> We have no lot in the son of Jesse.
> Away to your homes, O Israel;
> now see to your own house, David.

So Israel went to their homes, and Rehoboam ruled
over those Israelites who lived in the cities of
Judah.

Then King Rehoboam sent out Adoram, the
commander of the forced levies, but the Israelites
stoned him to death; thereupon King Rehoboam
mounted his chariot in haste and fled to Jerusalem.
From that day to this, the whole of Israel has been
in rebellion against the house of David.

When the men of Israel heard that Jeroboam
had returned, they sent and called him to the
assembly and made him king over the whole of
Israel. The tribe of Judah alone followed the house
of David. (I Kings 12: 1-20)

In terms of contemporary politics the fall of Samaria was a
considerable event, considerable enough at least to find a
place in the annals of its conqueror Sargon. The kings had
been powerful monarchs and the kings of Babylon and of
Egypt had at least taken them seriously. With Judah it was

quite otherwise. She was the junior partner, dragged unwillingly along, only too often in the wake of the northern king's policy. But at least Judah survived, a tiny enclave now, part of the massive Assyrian empire with no prospect of greatness and always at the mercy of the next conqueror with dreams of world-wide hegemony. The inhabitants of Judah, however, whilst trembling for their own fate when Samaria fell, were able in some senses to shrug off the challenge which it represented to them. Could not the fall of Samaria be regarded as a judgment upon the northern kingdom for its secession from the Davidic monarchy? Had not Jeroboam established schismatic shrines in the northern kingdom and provided for worship the abhorred bull calf symbols roundly condemned in the Torah?

> Then Jeroboam rebuilt Shechem in the hill-country of Ephraim and took up residence there; from there he went out and built Penuel. "As things now stand," he said to himself, "the kingdom will revert to the house of David. If this people go up to sacrifice in the house of the Lord in Jerusalem, it will revive their allegiance to their lord Rehoboam king of Judah, and they will kill me and return to King Rehoboam." After giving thought to the matter he made two calves of gold and said to the people, "It is too much trouble for you to go up to Jerusalem; here are your gods, Israel, that brought you up from Egypt." One he set up at Bethel and the other he put at Dan, and this thing became a sin in Israel; the people went to Bethel to worship the one, and all the way to Dan to worship the other. He set up shrines on the hill-tops also and appointed priests from every class of the people, who did not belong to the Levites. He instituted a pilgrim-feast on the fifteenth day of the eighth month like that in Judah, and he offered sacrifices upon the altar. This he did at Bethel, sacrificing to the calves that he had made and compelling the priests of the hill-shrines, which he had set up, to serve at Bethel.' (I Kings 12: 25-32)

Thus, those who viewed the discomfiture of Samaria from afar could take some comfort from the thought that the kingdom had perished for lack of loyalty to the truly anointed king of the house of Judah and for lack of obedience to the sacred Torah of Moses. Given the simplistic view widely accepted in that day, that disaster followed upon moral obloquy, it was possible to account for the disappearance from the face of the earth of the ten tribes of Israel. But at least Judah remained, holding fast to the divinely appointed monarchy and to the divinely appointed law. They were small, they were vulnerable, they were of no consequence in the eyes of the nations of the world, but they were God's people, worshipping Him on the Holy hill of Zion, observing His law and obeying His king. So they remained for nearly 150 years. They survived invasion, famine, economic disaster, political division, because they were God's people. This is Isaiah prophesying only twenty years after the fall of Samaria when Judah itself was smitten by those same Assyrian armies.

> Shame upon those who go down to Egypt for
>   help
>   and rely on horses,
>   putting their trust in chariots many in number
>   and in horsemen in their thousands,
>   but do not look to the Holy One of Israel
>   or seek guidance of the LORD!
> Yet the LORD too in his wisdom can bring about
>   trouble
>   and he does not take back his words;
>   he will rise up against the league of evildoers,
>   against all who help those who do wrong.
>   The Egyptians are men, not God,
>   their horses are flesh, not spirit;
>   and, when the LORD stretches out his hand,
> the helper will stumble and he who is helped will
>   fall,
>   and they will all vanish together.

This is what the LORD has said to me:

As a lion or a young lion growls over its prey
when the muster of shepherds is called out against
        it,
   and is not scared at their noise
   or cowed by their clamour,
so shall the LORD of Hosts come down to do battle
  for Mount Zion and her high summit.
Thus the LORD of Hosts, like a bird hovering
        over its young,
  will be a shield over Jerusalem;
   he will shield her and deliver her,
   standing over her and delivering her.
O Israel, come back to him whom you have so
        deeply offended,
  for on that day when you spurn, one and all,
  the idols of silver and the idols of gold
  which your own sinful hands have made,
Assyria shall fall by the sword, but by no sword of
        man;
  a sword that no man wields shall devour him.
He shall flee before the sword,
  and his young warriors shall be put to forced
        labour,
  his officers shall be helpless from terror
  and his captains too dismayed to flee.
  This is the very word of the LORD
  whose fire blazes in Zion,
  and whose furnace is set up in Jerusalem.
                     (Isa. 31)

Yes, the Lord was like a lion guarding his prey, He was a shield over Jerusalem. It was a sublime faith which the prophet Isaiah thus expressed and it was a faith shared, though in varying degrees, by those to whom he spoke. Disasters always happen to other people. But in the end disaster was to fall upon Judah. In 597 B.C. the kingdom was ravaged by the Babylonian army and many of its leaders were taken into exile. But worse was to follow—in 586 Jerusalem was destroyed, its temple was burnt, the walls were razed and the Davidic monarchy ceased from the face of the earth. Evil-merodach, King of Babylon, treated Jehoiachin, King of Judah, kindly but it was the kindness of a conqueror who had nothing to fear from the tiny kingdom of Judah.

> In the thirty-seventh year of the exile of Jehoiachin king of Judah, on the twenty-seventh day of the twelfth month, Evil-merodach king of Babylon in the year of his accession showed favour to Jehoiachin king of Judah. He brought him out of prison, treated him kindly and gave him a seat at table above the kings with him in Babylon. So Jehoiachin discarded his prison clothes and lived as a pensioner of the king for the rest of his life. For his maintenance, a regular daily allowance was given him by the king as long as he lived. (II Kings 25: 27-30)

The fall of Samaria could be viewed as the judgment of God upon an apostate nation. But what were the prophets and historians of the exile to make of the fall of Judah? We must not exaggerate. The whole population was not deported and there were some zealous spirits still to be found amongst the exiles. Life could be tolerable and indeed many Jews in Babylon rose to high office and achieved a certain affluence. They did not all hang up their harps. There proved to be some who were capable of singing the Lord's song even in a strange land. But the identity of the nation and its corporate role in God's purposes was now wholly uncertain. The Davidic monarchy was no more, although it had been established, so it was believed, at the direct command of God to Samuel. The temple worship in Jerusalem was in abeyance, although commanded for all eternity by God in the wilderness. What was left, therefore, which could constitute Judah a peculiar people? This was a painful question and as it happened, on the answer to it depended the direction which a large part of mankind was ultimately to take. There was only one answer immediately to hand. Yes, Jerusalem had been taken, the Ark of the Lord had been lost, the sacrifices had been suspended and the king was no more, but they did have "the law"—not indeed any longer available on the tablets of stone but by now written on the heart of many an Israelite in a foreign land and in some form constituting part of the sacred writings of the people. Samaria had fallen not just as a result of political mismanagement but, so it was believed, because of their flagrant disregard of the law of God. Judah had fallen not just because of the foolish fluctuating policies of their leaders but because she too had disregarded the law of God. Had not the prophets warned them that it would be so?

These were the words of the Lord: Go down to the house of the king of Judah and say this: Listen to the words of the Lord, O king of Judah, you who sit on David's throne, you and your courtiers and your people who come in at these gates. These are the words of the Lord: Deal justly and fairly, rescue the victim from his oppressor, do not ill-treat or do violence to the alien, the orphan or the widow, do not shed innocent blood in this place. If you obey, and only if you obey, kings who sit on David's throne shall yet come riding through these gates in chariots and on horses, with their retinue of courtiers and people. But if you do not listen to my words, then by myself I swear, says the Lord, this house shall become a desolate ruin. For these are the words of the Lord about the royal house of Judah:

Though you are dear to me as Gilead
    or as the heights of Lebanon,
I swear that I will make you a wilderness,
    a land of unpeopled cities.
I will dedicate an armed host to fight against you,
    a ravening horde;
they shall cut your choicest cedars down
    and fling them on the fire.

Men of many nations shall pass by this city and say to one another, "Why has the Lord done this to such a great city?" The answer will be, "Because they foresook their covenant with the Lord their

God; they worshipped other gods and served them."
(Jer. 22: 1-9)

The argument could lead to only one conclusion—it was the
law of God which now constituted the identity of the true
Israel and obedience to it was to be the mark of their
nationhood and the means of their salvation. We are already
in the presence of that theological conviction which our Lord
and St. Paul were to encounter in all its rigour five hundred
years later. It was the natural, perhaps indeed the only
possible, reaction to the devastating impact of the year 586
B.C. We still feel the shock waves of that event in the
Christian Church today and in our relationships with modern
Judaism. 586 B.C. was infinitely more significant in the
history of the world than A.D. 1066 in the life of Britain. To
Nebuchadnezzar, that crude brutal monarch of the ancient
world, the little kingdom of Judah was no more than a flea
under his foot. But when he burnt the temple and razed the
walls, and carried off a few more defeated enemies to Babylon
he released powers which challenge and dominate us still. He
ensured the dissemination of the law of God throughout the
world and many a Jonah would be born to trouble the mighty
self-sufficient kingdoms of antiquity.

But I leap ahead too fast. For the moment we must content
ourselves with more pedestrian progress and see what may be
deduced from the documents of the Old Testament which
relate to, or arise from, the period after the disaster. I put it in
that rather deliberate way because the reader will have to
grow accustomed to the fact that a distinction has to be made
between the events being described and the situation of the
person describing them. It is important in the New
Testament, for example, to ask not simply what the events of
our Lord's life meant but what they meant in the mind of the
person relating them and in the mind of the congregation
receiving them. To take a more up-to-date example, a war
correspondent's dispatches from the front will tell you
something about the events on that front but it will also tell
you something about the war correspondent himself and
about the temper of the people to whom he sends his
dispatches. Do they need to be encouraged with news of
victory, or do they need to be challenged with news of the cost

of victory in terms of men and materials? But the editor's judgment may vary from that of his correspondent. Again, the final result as it appears in the newspaper will be telling us something not only about the front and about the war correspondent but what the editor thinks about the people who will be reading his newspaper. That is a somewhat elaborate analogy but I hope not unhelpful in studying the documents of the Old Testament. For there is little doubt that most of the documents of the Old Testament achieved their final shape and developed into a corporate body of literature in the period after the exile and under the influence of the appalling events associated with the year 586. I doubt if we shall ever know what part of the Torah went with the exiles into Babylon but most scholars still incline to the view that those documents were organised and rounded off by the scribes of the exilic period who, after all, had little else to do. Even the prophetic writings arising indubitably out of the period of the monarchy probably reached their final shape and achieved a certain status during the exile. The "writings" are almost by definition late, viz. Chronicles, Ezra, Nehemiah, Daniel, Esther, and many of the so-called apocryphal books date from the years immediately preceding the birth of Christ. The Old Testament, therefore, with which we are familiar as an organised group of writings, identifiable as "Sacred Scripture" and enjoying a certain prestige in the minds of the people, is the product of a period in Israel's history controlled and dominated by the collapse of Judah. Those documents will tell us a great deal, therefore, not only about the events they actually describe but about the attitudes of those who describe them and about the situation of "the public" for whom they were designed. The compilers and editors of the post-exilic period were not writing for posterity as they saw it but for the people amongst whom they lived. To put it another way, those writings have a certain apologetic purpose, designed to encourage or to challenge, to embolden or to condemn those who now constituted the Israel of God. The war correspondent's dispatch will no doubt be there in its original form but is heavily conditioned by the context in which it is printed and by the editorial which accompanies it. In the Old Testament we are in the presence of news and views.

If, now, we confine our attention to the literature of the
Old Testament as we have it, a reasonably coherent pattern
emerges. Most of us will be familiar with it and indeed most
of us have been taught it, but the reader at this point needs to
be warned that this stereotype is likely to be heavily qualified
by what he reads in the next chapter. Here it is, however, for
what it is worth. The story begins in 539 with an account of a
partial return to Jerusalem in the first year of Cyrus, king of
Persia.

> Now in the first year of Cyrus king of Persia, so
> that the word of the Lord spoken through Jeremiah
> might be fulfilled, the Lord stirred up the heart of
> Cyrus king of Persia; and he issued a proclamation
> throughout his kingdom, both by word of mouth
> and in writing, to this effect:
>
>> This is the word of Cyrus king of Persia: The
>> Lord the God of heaven has given me all the
>> kingdoms of the earth, and he himself has
>> charged me to build him a house at Jerusalem
>> in Judah. To every man of his people now among
>> you I say, God be with him, and let him go up to
>> Jerusalem in Judah, and rebuild the house of the
>> Lord the God of Israel, the God whose city is
>> Jerusalem. And every remaining Jew, wherever
>> he may be living, may claim aid from his neigh-
>> bours in that place, silver and gold, goods and
>> cattle, in addition to the voluntary offerings for
>> the house of God in Jerusalem.
>
> Thereupon the heads of families of Judah and
> Benjamin, and the priests and the Levites, answered
> the summons, all whom God had moved to go up to
> rebuild the house of the Lord in Jerusalem. Their
> neighbours all assisted them with gifts of every
> kind, silver and gold, goods and cattle and valuable
> gifts in abundance, in addition to any voluntary
> service. Moreover, Cyrus king of Persia produced
> the vessels of the house of the Lord which
> Nebuchadnezzar had removed from Jerusalem and

placed in the temple of his god; and he handed them over into the charge of Mithredath the treasurer, who made an inventory of them for Sheshbazzar the ruler of Judah. This was the list: thirty gold basins, a thousand silver basins, twenty-nine vessels of various kinds, thirty golden bowls, four hundred and ten silver bowls of various types, and a thousand other vessels. The vessels of gold and silver amounted in all to five thousand four hundred; and Sheshbazzar took them all up to Jerusalem, when the exiles were brought back from Babylon. (Ezra 1)

Subsequently, in the reign of Artaxerxes, the returned exiles were joined by Ezra.

Now after these events, in the reign of Artaxerxes king of Persia, there came up from Babylon one Ezra son of Seraiah, son of Azariah, son of Hilkiah, son of Shallum, son of Zadok, son of Ahitub, son of Amariah, son of Azariah, son of Meraioth, son of Zerahiah, son of Uzzi, son of Bukki, son of Abishua, son of Phinehas, son of Eleazar, son of Aaron the chief priest. He was a scribe learned in the law of Moses which the Lord the God of Israel had given them; and the king granted him all that he asked, for the hand of the Lord his God was upon him. In the seventh year of King Artaxerxes, other Israelites, priests, Levites, singers, door-keepers, and temple-servitors went up with him to Jerusalem; and they reached Jerusalem in the fifth month, in the seventh year of the king. On the first day of the first month Ezra fixed the day for departure from Babylon, and on the first day of the fifth month he arrived at Jerusalem, for the gracious hand of his God was upon him. For Ezra had devoted himself to the study and observance of the law of the Lord and to teaching statute and ordinance in Israel. (Ezra 7: 1-10)

The story becomes confused at this point because scholars are far from being able to establish the historical relationship between Ezra and Nehemiah. "Which came first?" the examiners ask—and the hapless examinees answer along the lines of the book they last read on the subject. We need not be detained by the argument for we are primarily concerned not with what happened but with the import of the books describing what happened. So I quote now from Nehemiah 8: 1-10:

> When the seventh month came, and the Israelites were now settled in their towns, the people assembled as one man in the square in front of the Water Gate, and Ezra the scribe was asked to bring the book of the law of Moses, which the Lord had enjoined upon Israel. On the first day of the seventh month, Ezra the priest brought the law before the assembly, every man and woman, and all who were capable of understanding what they heard. He read from it, facing the square in front of the Water Gate, from early morning till noon, in the presence of the men and the women, and those who could understand; all the people listened attentively to the book of the law. Ezra the scribe stood on a wooden platform made for the purpose, and beside him stood Mattithiah, Shema, Anaiah, Uriah, Hilkiah, and Maaseiah on his right hand; and on his left Pedaiah, Mishael, Malchiah, Hashum, Hashbaddanah, Zechariah and Meshullam. Ezra opened the book in the sight of all the people, for he was standing above them; and when he opened it, they all stood. Ezra blessed the Lord, the great God, and all the people raised their hands and answered, 'Amen, Amen'; and they bowed their heads and prostrated themselves humbly before the Lord. Jeshua, Bani, Sherebiah, Jamin, Akkub, Shabbethai, Hodiah, Maaseiah, Kelita, Azariah, Jozabad, Hanan, Pelaiah, the Levites, expounded the law to the people while they remained in their places. They read from the book of the law of God clearly, made its sense plain and gave instruction in what was read.

Then Nehemiah the governor and Ezra the priest and scribe, and the Levites who instructed the people, said to them all, "This day is holy to the Lord your God; do not mourn or weep." For all the people had been weeping while they listened to the words of the law. Then he said to them, "You may go now; refresh yourselves with rich food and sweet drinks, and send a share to all who cannot provide for themselves; for this day is holy to our Lord. Let there be no sadness, for joy in the Lord is your strength."

The situation which the chronicler (author of the books of Ezra and Nehemiah) wishes us to understand is well delineated and coherent and it is this. By the hand of God, in accordance with the prophecy of Jeremiah, the heathen kings of Persia were moved to permit a return to Jerusalem and indeed made lavish provision for that return out of government funds. Thus it was that the walls of Jerusalem were rebuilt, the temple ruins were reconsecrated and sacrifices were resumed. But these were not the most significant events. At the heart of them is the somewhat mysterious figure of Ezra "a ready scribe in the law of Moses" who made it his life's work to re-establish the law of God in Jerusalem among the exiles who had returned from Babylon. "Ezra had devoted himself to the study and observance of the law of the Lord and to teaching statute and ordinance in Israel" (Ezra 7: 10). The Christian reader at this point tends to leap from the end of the fifth century B.C. to the first century A.D. and to supply what is missing from the text by his own imagination. So he envisages the city of Jerusalem rebuilt, the temple *cultus* restored, scribes diligently at work and the people somewhat reluctantly knuckling down to the job of observing an ever-growing number of domestic, social and cultic regulations which to his mind comprises the Judaism of Our Lord's day. This view of things is sustained from the pages of the New Testament by the account of Our Lord's seeming conflict with law and Paul's scathing attacks on it and on those who prescribed it. The woes upon the Pharisees echo in our minds; we rejoice in the freedom we have discovered through Paul from the painful inhibiting strait-jacket of Jewish legalism. The centuries between Ezra and Paul vanish as a dream and the modern pilgrim looks at the walls he thinks Nehemiah built and imagines our Lord calling down doom upon them. Demolish the walls of the great institution, we say; take down the tablets from behind the altar. Man is come of age and he may safely move out from within the walls which Nehemiah built and from the stuffy cage in which Ezra incarcerated his people.

I warned you that this was to be a stereotype—and so it is. It rests too heavily upon the documents of the Old Testament with which we are familiar and takes too little account even of the so-called apocryphal writing, and even less account of the extra-biblical material which is available to us. The stereotype is correct in what it asserts but misleading because of what it omits. It is to what is omitted that I turn in the next chapter.

We were never more free than under the German occupation ... at each moment we were living to the full the meaning of that banal little phrase: "All men are mortal". The choice that each of us made of himself was authentic, because it was made in the presence of death, since it could always be expressed in the form, "Rather death than—."

Sartre
Situations

VIII

The Jews Abroad

Embedded within the pages of Ezra and Nehemiah there are certain sections which purport to be memoirs narrated in the first person. There is no particular reason to doubt that they represent what we might call, on the basis of a previous analogy, "front line dispatches". After all, Ezra and Nehemiah were in the front line trying to restore the morale of a despondent people behind the broken walls of the city and around the fire-darkened ruins of the temple. There is a sense in which both Ezra and Nehemiah were "natives" of Babylon, by then part of a substantial community, probably more numerous than the Jewish community in Judah. Ezra had a professional position as scribe, and Nehemiah was an important official in the Royal Court. They were not, distinctly not, on the breadline as their brothers were in the homeland. Like many a Jewish émigré in New York at the beginning of this century, it was a pleasing sentiment to be associated with the promised land but few of the exiles in Babylon would have been willing to return to it. Here then is a section from the memoirs of Nehemiah, vividly written, in which the contrast between his own life in Babylon and the precarious existence of his brothers in Judea, is only too painfully obvious.

> Now I was the king's cupbearer, and one day, in the month Nisan, in the twentieth year of King Artaxerxes, when his wine was ready, I took it up and handed it to the king, and as I stood before him I was feeling very unhappy. He said to me, "Why do you look so unhappy? You are not ill; it can be nothing but unhappiness." I was much afraid and answered, "The king will live for ever. But how can I help looking unhappy when the city where my forefathers are buried lies waste and its gates

are burnt?" "What are you asking of me?" said the king. I prayed to the God of heaven, and then I answered, "If it please your majesty, and if I enjoy your favour, I beg you to send me to Judah, to the city where my forefathers are buried, so that I may rebuild it." The king, with the queen consort sitting beside him, asked me, "How long will the journey last and when will you return?" Then the king approved the request and let me go, and I told him how long I should be. Then I said to the king, "If it please your majesty, let letters be given me for the governors in the province of Beyond-Euphrates with orders to grant me all the help I need for my journey to Judah. Let me have also a letter for Asaph, the keeper of your royal forests, instructing him to supply me with timber to make beams for the gates of the citadel, which adjoins the palace, and for the city wall, and for the palace which I shall occupy." The king granted my requests, for the gracious hand of my God was upon me. I came in due course to the governors in the province of Beyond-Euphrates and presented to them the king's letters; the king had given me an escort of army officers with cavalry. But when Sanballat the Horonite and the slave Tobiah, an Ammonite, heard this, they were much vexed that someone should have come to promote the interests of the Israelites.

When I arrived in Jerusalem, I waited three days. Then I set out by night, taking a few men with me; but I told no one what my God was prompting me to do for Jerusalem. I had no beast with me except the one on which I myself rode. I went out by night through the Valley Gate towards the Dragon Spring and the Dung Gate, and I inspected the places where the walls of Jerusalem had been broken down and her gates burnt. Then I passed on to the Fountain Gate and the King's Pool; but there was no room for me to ride through. I went up the valley in the night and inspected the city wall; then I re-entered the city by the Valley

Gate. So I arrived back without the magistrates knowing where I had been or what I was doing. I had not yet told the Jews, the priests, the nobles, the magistrates, or any of those who would be responsible for the work.

Then I said to them, "You see our wretched plight. Jerusalem lies in ruins, its gates destroyed by fire. Come let us rebuild the wall of Jerusalem and be rid of the reproach." I told them how the gracious hand of my God had been upon me and also what the king had said to me. They replied, "Let us start the rebuilding." So they set about the work vigorously and to good purpose. (Neh. 2: 1-18)

If we had only the memoirs of Ezra and Nehemiah we would still have to say that the events in which they were involved were highly significant for the future of Israel and indeed for the future of the world. Without those two men and the inflexible purpose they brought to their task it is difficult to see how the remnant in Judea could have survived. There would have been no "Holy Land"; the city, such of it as remained, would have been peopled by men of mixed race; temple ritual would not have been restored and there would have been no particular reason why the future of Israel should have been associated with Jerusalem. But we cannot, as Bible readers are apt to do, move straight from the stirring account of Israel's restoration in Judea as it is recorded in Ezra and Nehemiah to the New Testament period. Nearly five hundred years of history lies in between. So whilst it is true that our Lord could have walked "through the Valley Gate towards the Dragon Spring and the Dung Gate [and] on to the Fountain Gate in the King's Pool" he would be walking in a city different in almost every other respect from that which Nehemiah recreated; he would have been part of a culture vastly different from that with which Nehemiah was familiar. So whilst there is obviously a clear connection between the events recorded in Ezra and Nehemiah's memoirs and the Israel of our Lord's day, it would be a gross mistake to assume a direct line of development. If you will pardon another analogy, you can travel on the Northern Line direct from High Barnet to Morden. But the underground map does not even begin to represent the two-lane highways and the narrow streets, the cul-de-sacs and the squares, the right hand turns and the devious routes, the squalors and the splendours which will confront the traveller who actually wishes to go by road from High Barnet to Morden. We shall have a very misleading picture of the history of this period if we simply go down the escalator in the time of Ezra and Nehemiah and emerge again in the time of John the Baptist.

We begin by observing that it is impossible to isolate the history and culture of Israel from the history and culture of the surrounding world. The founding of Rome, if the traditional date is accepted, is contemporary with the prophecies of Amos. Ezekiel was a contemporary of Pythagoras; whilst Ezra was reading his laws to the people of Jerusalem, Euripides was writing his plays for the people of Athens. The writers of the so-called Priestly Code were busy about their work when Plato was constructing the *Republic.* It is part of the genius of the Hebraic/Christian faith that it is bedded in with the battles and treaties, the theatres and academies, the poetry and drama, social customs and the political junketings of the ancient world. The memoirs of Ezra and Nehemiah seem to relate to distinct identifiable moments in the life of Israel and are not associated by their authors with the general history of the period. But these memoirs are of course only part of the Books Ezra and Nehemiah—and the Books of Ezra and Nehemiah themselves are only part of a much larger work attributed, for lack of any more positive identification, to an author called "The Chronicler". May I repeat a point which was made in the previous chapter, that we have to make a distinction between dispatches from the front representing the views of the correspondent on the spot and those same dispatches as they are incorporated in a newspaper some weeks later, or in an authoritative history some centuries later. In each case the presentation will depend not simply upon the events being described but upon the attitudes respectively of the war correspondent, the editor and the author, who themselves will be affected by the cultural climate of their own time, and no less by the readership they have in mind. The biographies I have on my shelves, e.g. on Disraeli, Campbell-Bannerman, Lloyd-George, Baldwin, Ramsay MacDonald, will enlighten me not only about those men and the events in which they were involved, but about the authors and the events in which *they* were involved. So it is not possible to judge even the memoirs of Ezra and Nehemiah without regard to the book of which they formed a part and the historical circumstance under which that book reached the public. The problem, as you might well expect by now, is that scholarly opinion is sharply divided as to the date of the Chronicler's book. It could have been anywhere between the latter part of the fourth century B.C. and the latter part of the second century B.C. We therefore have to allow for a wide latitude in time and correspondingly a wide latitude in interpretation. The only thing we can say with certainty is that the book saw the light of day and became familiar to the people of Israel in the so-called Greek period.

The Greeks had long been, in one sense at least, the intellectual masters of the world, but the Greek period proper begins in the year 336 B.C. when Alexander the Great, son of Philip, pupil of Aristotle, succeeded to the throne of Macedonia after the assassination of his father. In 335 he destroyed Thebes but (characteristically) spared Athens. He defeated Darius the great king in 333 and marched on India in 326. The empire he founded was of short duration and after his death it broke up rapidly under the pressures of the rivalries amongst those who succeeded him. But his influence upon subsequent history proved stupendous. He was not just a military genius. He was a pupil of Aristotle and was possessed of a burning zeal for the dissemination of Greek culture. He was not just an empire builder; he was an evangelist. I know of no better introduction to what we may call the Greek view of life than that which is quoted in *The Harvest of Hellenism* by F. E. Peters (Simon and Schuster 1970). Here it is from the funeral oration delivered by Pericles at Athens in the year 429 not long after Nehemiah rebuilt the walls of Jerusalem.

> Our political system is called a democracy because the rule is not in the hands of a few but under the control of the majority. In private disputes everyone stands equal before the law, while in questions of public preferment it is merit rather than class membership that is esteemed. Poverty is

no bar to public service; whoever has some good to perform for the polis is recognized.

Our private lives are conducted with the same openness as our public business; and every man is free to enjoy himself in the manner he wishes without provoking the anger of his neighbor or receiving those offensive glances which, though they do no real harm, cause grief. Private freedom is not public license; we reverence and obey the law. We obey both the authorities and the authority of the laws, especially those laws designed to protect the wronged and the unwritten laws which possess the sanction of public shame.

When our work is over we recreate our spirits in the public contests and religious festivals which fill the polis year. There are private delights as well, pursued with moderation and good taste, whose pleasures draw away our daily cares. Because of the greatness of our polis the goods of the world come home to us, and we enjoy them naturally as our own.

Our love of the beautiful is unmarred by extravagance, and our pursuit of the things of the mind has not led us into softness. We use our wealth for practical ends rather than as a subject for boasting. We do not consider a man's poverty a shameful thing; the disgrace is in doing nothing to avoid it. We have an equal concern for our home and our polis, and even those of us who are chiefly engaged in business have a profound knowledge of politics. We alone have no respect for a man disinterested in political life. He is not minding his business; he rather is thought to be useless. We are the judges of our own actions and give careful thought to our affairs. For us discussion is no bar to action; what is harmful is to act before submitting a policy to discussion. We are unusual in that we are capable of taking risks even after we have weighed their consequences, while other men are brave as long as they are ignorant but draw back upon reflection.

Taken all in all, this polis is the school of Hellas.
Each citizen is master of his own person in all
circumstances and is so with exceeding grace and
versatility.

It would be difficult to find a more humane, civilised,
imaginative view of life than the one which is reflected in this
magnificent oration. Aristotle conveyed its spirit faithfully to
his pupil and two thousand five hundred years later we still
live under its spell. This is the kind of life we would like to
live, this is the kind of political system which we could
applaud, this is an objective for the human race to which we
could give our hearts and our minds. Most of the
characteristic institutions of the twentieth century owe their
origins and ethos to this view of life. In one form or another it
dominates our educational system, prescribes our social
objectives and mocks our attempt to improve on it. We are all
Hellenists at heart whether we are Capitalists or Marxists,
Christians or Pagans.

Do I seem to digress? Or revel again in those first
impressions of Greek life and literature which were imparted
to me at school? I shall only seem to digress if you are still
captured by the stereotype which I described in the last
chapter—which itself arises out of a very partialist bit of
history and an unprofitable kind of biblicism. For the fact of
the matter is that the Jews from the fall of Jerusalem
onwards lived inescapably in an environment largely shaped
and coloured by Greek culture. Long before Alexander
embarked upon his conquest of the world Greek culture and
Greek language were making their way along the trade
routes, the diplomatic channels and the corridors of power.
Greek values were being transmitted in Greek-style schools
and academies. It was the culture of the educated man. It is
important to bear in mind that even before the fall of
Jerusalem there were large communities of Jews living
outside Judah—in Alexandria and Elephantine, in Antioch
and Aleppo, in Nippur and Ecbatana; Jonah could very well
have had relatives in Tarshish. Some Jews served as mer-
cenaries in foreign armies and were highly regarded for their
military prowess. By the end of the period we are concerned
with they could be found as far afield as Carthage, Sardinia

and Spain. In 270 B.C. the Egyptian government settled thirty thousand Jews on the Sinai frontier as a protection against invasion. Population figures for the ancient world are notoriously difficult to arrive at but *The Jewish People* by Harry Shapiro (Unesco) estimates a total Jewish population in the world at the beginning of the Christian era at about four million. It could be that by then three million of them were living elsewhere than in the homeland. So it was not only by the waters of Babylon that they sat down and wept. Some of them were not weeping either—they had good jobs, they were well educated, they occupied positions of power in foreign governments, they were generals in mercenary armies. No doubt, to the Jews of the homeland the Jews of the Diaspora were exiles suffering in some far outpost of the Greek Empire; but the exiles themselves had a rather different view and were secretly somewhat contemptuous of the cousins labouring in some poor upland farm in Judea or making a precarious living as a cobbler in a city street. Rich men pursue their genealogies and indulge a taste for nostalgia in the village of their forefathers—but are glad enough to go "home" again to the heated apartment and the big car and the plush business premises.

Let us then for a moment forget the homeland and the memoirs of Ezra and Nehemiah, so narrowly concerned with that homeland, and imagine ourselves in the Diaspora, living in a Greek city, fighting in a Greek mercenary army, working for a Greek employer, teaching in a Greek school, part of the staff in the great library at Alexandria, playing in the local orchestra. I am of course acquainted with the history of my race; my father or the local rabbi will have seen to that. I am aware that I am a member of a peculiar people who seem to have a special role in the world and live by standards uncomfortably different from the boys I mix with at school or the men I work with in the office. I have to speak Greek if I am to make any progress and my knowledge of Hebrew is scanty. My father tells me about the Torah of God by which I am to rule my life, but to tell the truth it seems to bear little relation to the life I actually live or to the friends with whom I mix. So, as the reverie might end—Why am I a Jew? What am I to do with my Jewishness? There are for any émigré roughly three ways of responding and these ways I now describe.

The obvious way is to assimilate to the culture in which I find myself; I go to the Greek school in the city rather than to the synagogue school in the village; I compete in the games at the gymnasium; I cut my hair short. If I live in Nippur or Ecbatana or Antioch I do not look any different from my fellow men apart from the marks of circumcision—but even those could be removed by the surgery of the day. I become, in short, a cultivated cosmopolitan Greek gentleman. The Torah remains part of my history but no longer controls my life. I make my own decisions on such ethical grounds as remain convincing to me. So Philo alludes to critics of the Torah in Greek-educated Jewish circles in Alexandria,

> who disregard kinsmen and friends, who transgress laws in which they were born and brought up, who undermine ancestral custom which cannot rightly be censured and fall away from it ... they proclaim their displeasure with the constitution made by the fathers and express incessant censure and complain against the law, talking about the ludicrous fables of the Pentateuch. (quoted in *Judaism and Hellenism* by Martin Hengel, SCM 1974)

But Martin Hengel acknowledges elsewhere in his book that "the Jews of the Diaspora remained, on the whole, constant in the face of these temptations". The English were not the first to insist on dressing for dinner in the jungle. The Diaspora Jew could adopt a quite different stance from the one that I have described above and assert not his identity with, but his alienation from, the culture in which he happens to live. Within the pages of Holy Scripture we have that attitude powerfully portrayed in the Book of Daniel which itself belongs to the Greek period. The author is writing about the third year of the reign of Jehoiakim, King of Judah in the sixth century but he is writing for those who are facing the allurements of Greek culture in the second century. The first chapter describes how four young men resisted the temptation of "unclean" food:

In the third year of the reign of Jehoiakim king of Judah came Nebuchadnezzar king of Babylon unto Jerusalem, and besieged it.

And the Lord gave Jehoiakim king of Judah into his hand, with part of the vessels of the house of God: which he carried into the land of Shinar to the house of his god; and he brought the vessels into the treasure house of his god.

And the king spake unto Ashpenaz the master of his eunuchs, that he should bring certain of the children of Israel, and of the king's seed, and of the princes;

Children in whom was no blemish, but well favoured, and skilful in all wisdom, and cunning in knowledge, and understanding science, and such as had ability in them to stand in the king's palace, and whom they might teach the learning and the tongue of the Chaldeans.

And the king appointed them a daily provision of the king's meat, and of the wine which he drank: so nourishing them three years, that at the end thereof they might stand before the king.

Now among these were of the children of Judah, Daniel, Hananiah, Mishael, and Azariah:

Unto whom the prince of the eunuchs gave names: for he gave unto Daniel the name of Belteshazzar; and to Hananiah, of Shadrach; and to Mishael, of Meshach; and to Azariah, of Abednego.

But Daniel purposed in his heart that he would not defile himself with the portion of the king's meat, nor with the wine which he drank: therefore he requested of the prince of the eunuchs that he might not defile himself.

Now God had brought Daniel into favour and tender love with the prince of the eunuchs.

And the prince of the eunuchs said unto Daniel, I fear my lord the king, who hath appointed your meat and your drink: for why should he see your faces worse liking than the children which are of your sort? then shall ye make me endanger my head to the king.

Then said Daniel to Melzar, whom the prince of the eunuchs had set over Daniel, Hananiah, Mishael, and Azariah,

Prove thy servants, I beseech thee, ten days; let them give us pulse to eat, and water to drink.

Then let our countenances be looked upon before thee, and the countenance of the children that eat of the portion of the king's meat: and as thou seest, deal with thy servants.

So he consented to them in this matter, and proved them ten days.

And at the end of ten days their countenances appeared fairer and fatter in flesh than all the children which did eat the portion of the king's meat.

Thus Melzar took away the portion of their meat, and the wine that they should drink: and gave them pulse. (Dan. 1: 1-16, AV)

Chapter three describes their refusal to worship the golden image which King Nebuchadnezzar had made:

Nebuchadnezzar the king made an image of gold, whose height was threescore cubits, and the breadth thereof six cubits: he set it up in the plain of Dura, in the province of Babylon.

Then Nebuchadnezzar the king sent to gather together the princes, the governors, and the captains, the judges, the treasurers, the counsellers, the sheriffs, and all the rulers of the provinces, to come to the dedication of the image which Nebuchadnezzar the king had set up.

Then the princes, the governors, and captains, the judges, the treasurers, the counsellers, the sheriffs, and all the rulers of the provinces, were gathered together unto the dedication of the image that Nebuchadnezzar the king had set up; and they stood before the image that Nebuchadnezzar had set up.

Then an herald cried aloud, To you, it is commanded, O people, nations, and languages.

That at what time ye hear the sound of the cornet, flute, harp, sackbut, psaltery, dulcimer, and all kinds of musick, ye fall down and worship the golden image that Nebuchadnezzar the king hath set up:

And whoso falleth not down and worshippeth shall the same hour be cast into the midst of a burning fiery furnace.

Therefore at that time, when all the people heard the sound of the cornet, flute, harp, sackbut, psaltery, and all kinds of musick, all the people, the nations, and the languages, fell down and worshipped the golden image that Nebuchadnezzar the king had set up.

Wherefore at that time certain Chaldeans came near, and accused the Jews.

They spake and said to the king Nebuchadnezzar, O king, live for ever.

Thou, O king, hast made a decree, that every man that shall hear the sound of the cornet, flute, harp, sackbut, psaltery, and dulcimer, and all kinds of musick, shall fall down and worship the golden image:

And whoso falleth not down and worshippeth, that he should be cast into the midst of a burning fiery furnace.

There are certain Jews whom thou hast set over the affairs of the province of Babylon, Shadrach, Meshach, and Abednego; these men, O king, have not regarded thee: they serve not thy gods, nor worship the golden image which thou hast set up.

Then Nebuchadnezzar in his rage and fury commanded to bring Shadrach, Meshach, and Abednego. Then they brought these men before the king.

Nebuchadnezzar spake and said unto them, Is it true, O Shadrach, Meshach, and Abednego, do not ye serve my gods, nor worship the golden image which I have set up?

Now if ye be ready that at what time ye hear the sound of the cornet, flute, harp, sackbut, psaltery, and dulcimer, and all kinds of musick, ye fall down and worship the image which I have made; well: but if ye worship not, ye shall be cast the same hour into the midst of a burning fiery furnace; and who is that God that shall deliver you out of my hands?

Shadrach, Meshach, and Abednego, answered and said to the king, O Nebuchadnezzar, we are not careful to answer thee in this matter.

If it be so, our God whom we serve is able to deliver us from the burning fiery furnace, and he will deliver us out of thine hand, O king.

But if not, be it known unto thee, O king, that we will not serve thy gods, nor worship the golden image which thou hast set up. (Dan. 3: 1-18, AV)

Thus there grew up in the Diaspora sharp divisions between those who adhered to the faith of their fathers and those who did not, those who entered fully into the life of the people around them and those who hid themselves away in the ghetto in order the better to practise the faith of their fathers, to eat kosher food, to study the Torah and to keep themselves unspotted from the world. But there is a third possibility which falls somewhere between the two. That possibility is represented within the pages of Scripture by the Book of Jonah. It is a book *about* Jonah, the prophet referred to in II Kings 14: 25, but it is a book *for* people of the Diaspora in the Greek period. The story of the book is familiar enough to us all. The message is not always so clear but it is roughly this—that the people of Israel have found themselves transported into a foreign land to which they were extremely reluctant to go (Jonah had wanted to go to Tarshish). But now they are in that foreign land, the author says they ought to use the disaster positively and proclaim the truth as they have received it from God. Their conquerors were not to be seen simply as enemies but as the children of God waiting only for the Torah in order to repent. So a whole extrabiblical literature grew up which sought to commend the sacred Scriptures and the Torah in particular to the Gentiles amongst whom they lived. One such adventurer in this field of ideas was Philo, an Alexandrian Jew and an older contemporary of Paul, who was regarded as the leader of the

Jewish community in Alexandria during the reign of the Emperor Gaius. He was a prolific writer, so perhaps I may be forgiven if I simply quote from the article about him in the *Dictionary of Christian Theology* (ed. Alan Richardson):

> He attempted in his voluminous works, of which about forty survive, all written in Greek, to give a reinterpretation of traditional Judaism in Hellenistic terms. His philosophy is a remarkable combination of Jewish monotheism, Platonic traits such as the doctrine of ideas, and the Stoic concept of the Logos immanent in the world and animating and directing it. He was not a heterodox Jew, and observed and reverenced the law, but he was anxious to reinterpret it, and while preserving its form to transmute its substance into general philosophical, moral and psychological truths, in accordance with a characteristically Hellenistic Jewish tendency observable in his predecessors, Aristobulus (second century B.C.) and Pseudo-Aristeas (c. 100 B.C.). In order to effect this he borrowed and developed from pagan Hellenistic literature the technique of allegorizing a sacred text, and applied it to the O.T. (mainly the Pentateuch).

Another exemplar is the author of The Wisdom of Solomon, also of Alexandria, but possibly a century earlier than Philo, whose objective was different, namely the bolstering up of the faith of his compatriots, but whose methods were the same, i.e. the use of familiar Greek categories to describe and commend traditional teaching of the Jewish fathers and of the Torah. It is not without significance that it was in Alexandria that the great work of translating the Hebrew Scriptures into Greek was undertaken in the third and second centuries B.C. This was due partly to the fact that many Alexandrian Jews no longer understood the Hebrew language but partly also because some Jews at least were possessed of an ambition that their friends and neighbours would share in the riches of the sacred Torah which God had provided not only for them but for all mankind.

The picture of the Diaspora we have received is a variegated picture but within it certainly there is room for those Jews who, as farmers, merchants and soldiers were—

> little different from the other easterners who had migrated from their homeland into the polis. The Jews were like their neighbors in all save their intransigent monotheism and their claim to an extraordinary document that provided an ideal and a norm for human behaviour. Other people possessed both myth and law describing their own past and regulating the conduct of society; the Jewish Torah was both of these, and more. It described the historical unfolding of God's providential plan for his own people and provided a code of conduct that had become, in recent times, the sole and authoritative basis of Jewish life. (Peters—*Harvest of Hellenism*)

Even the author of Ecclesiastes, notable for his lack of reference to the historic and religious foundations of his race, and despite his seeming surrender to the Greek view of life, does not altogether yield to its fascination. If the last chapter may be safely attributed to the author of the rest of the book (as I believe it can) the author remains, in his own diminished way, a believer in God and an observer of God's Torah.

> Remember now thy Creator in the days of thy youth, while the evil days come not, nor the years draw nigh, when thou shalt say, I have no pleasure in them;
>
> While the sun, or the light, or the moon, or the stars, be not darkened, nor the clouds return after the rain:
>
> In the day when the keepers of the house shall tremble, and the strong men shall bow themselves, and the grinders cease because they are few, and those that look out of the windows be darkened,
>
> And the doors shall be shut in the streets, when the sound of the grinding is low, and he shall rise

up at the voice of the bird, and all the daughters of
musick shall be brought low;

Also when they shall be afraid of that which is
high, and fears shall be in the way, and the almond
tree shall flourish, and the grasshopper shall be a
burden, and desire shall fail: because man goeth to
his long home, and the mourners go about the
streets:

Or ever the silver cord be loosed, or the golden
bowl be broken, or the pitcher be broken at the
fountain, or the wheel broken at the cistern.

Then shall the dust return to the earth as it was:
and the spirit shall return unto God who gave it.

Vanity of vanities, saith the preacher; all is
vanity.

And moreover, because the preacher was wise, he
still taught the people knowledge; yea, he gave good
heed, and sought out, and set in order many
proverbs.

The preacher sought to find out acceptable
words: and that which was written was upright,
even words of truth.

The words of the wise are as goads, and as nails
fastened by the masters of assemblies, which are
given from one shepherd.

And further, by these, my son, be admonished: of
making many books there is no end; and much
study is a weariness of the flesh.

Let us hear the conclusion of the whole matter:
Fear God, and keep his commandments; for this is
the whole duty of man.

For God shall bring every work into judgment,
with every secret thing, whether it be good, or
whether it be evil. (Ecclesiastes 12, AV)

At that stage in the history of the Greek period in which Paul
lived, he was able to travel round the Diaspora and to find
groups of Jews everywhere living by the Torah and even
making converts among the Gentiles around them.

Given the fact that maybe as much as three-quarters of
Jewry lived outside Palestine, we have yet to attend to the

other quarter who maintained, or at some stage resumed, their residence there. Jerusalem was not one of the cultural centres of the ancient world; it was not, on the whole, a meeting place for the nations, and it therefore enjoyed a certain immunity to fashion and custom which was not possible for those who lived cheek by jowl with their Gentile neighbours in the Diaspora.

But we must not press the contrast too far, and I myself am greatly indebted to Martin Hengel in his two-volume work *Judaism and Hellenism* for keeping the record straight. Anyone who wishes to know in detail the history of the period immediately preceding the coming of Christ could well make himself familiar with this book. I content myself with a few observations. I was surprised, for example, on a recent visit to the Holy Land to find the signs of the Zodiac used as a decoration on the floor of an ancient synagogue in Lower Galilee. I was surprised to realise not very long ago that an old and revered member of the Sanhedrin in the time of our Lord had a Greek name—Nicodemus (conqueror of the people). We still cannot be sure, after centuries of scholarship, that Jesus of Nazareth did not himself speak Greek and certainly some of His disciples had Greek names. These are the visible remains of a long and painful conflict which convulsed even Palestinian Judaism during the Greek period. I quote from Martin Hengel's book, page 49:

> With the coming of the Ptolemaic "economic and social policy", the social conflict which Nehemiah in his time strove to obviate must have grown substantially more acute, especially as religious motives were at work here. The new masters relied on the support of the "nobles and officials", the aristocratic estate-owners and the leaders of the priesthood, on whom Nehemiah had delivered such a sharp judgment one hundred and fifty years before. In these circles the dominant attitude was one of resistance to the reforms of Nehemiah and Ezra together with the growing legal rigorism and separatism that these produced. Although this group could not make headway against the majority of the people, they never gave up contact with

avowed opponents of reform, the house of Sanballat in Samaria and the "Ammonite" Tobiads. That now, in contrast to Persian times, they gained influence, is shown by the kinship of Tobias with the high priest and the move of the Tobiad family to Jerusalem, attested by Josephus. These circles sought the profitable contact with the "foreigners", whether these were Phoenician merchants or Greeks, which was so strongly attacked in Proverbs and also in Ben Sira. From here, too, there probably came those who were responsible for collecting tax: the leading priestly families appointed the officials of the temple treasury, like that Hezekiah who emigrated to Egypt in the time of Ptolemy I and whose "incomparable business efficiency", eloquence and close contact with the Greeks are so praised by Ps.-Hecataeus. The priests and lay nobility also had the possibility of leasing all kinds of duties; the Ptolemaic tax system was many-sided enough. In addition, good relations were maintained with the leading men in Alexandria, as is shown by the example of Tobias, his son Joseph, and perhaps also the Simon who is mentioned above.

On both economic-social and religious grounds, a development is beginning here which carried within itself the germ of conflicts. A relatively small, but rich and powerful upper class, which moreover had the confidence of their Greek masters and their immediate neighbours, faced on the one hand the representatives of a theocracy faithful to the Law, which was predominantly recruited from the lower priesthood and the Levites and whose conservative, legalistic and cultic attitude is manifested above all in the work of the Chronicler and those who revised it, together with Ben Sira, and on the other those groups in which the prophetic tradition lived on and apocalyptic was coming to birth.

So it was the upper classes and the rich aristocracy of Jerusalem which had most to gain from the Greek ascen-

dancy and sought most eagerly an accommodation with it.
They even seem to have sent their children away to school;
they conversed in Greek; they aped their style of dress, and
despised those rough and ready warriors of the law who
threatened the comfortable balance of power that had been
achieved.

We are now in a better position to understand the Books of
Ezra and Nehemiah. They are indeed *about* Ezra and
Nehemiah but they are *for* the author's fellow-countrymen of
the Greek period. Nehemiah indeed struggled with those
"who had married women from Ashdod, Ammon and Moab,
whose children spoke the language of Ashdod or of the other
peoples and could not speak the language of the Jews". The
walls of Jerusalem and the sacred "fence of the Torah" were
there to keep the Greeks at bay, not just the Samaritans, or
the Ammonites, or the Moabites.

> On that day they read in the book of Moses in
> the audience of the people; and therein was found
> written, that the Ammonite and the Moabite should
> not come into the congregation of God for ever;
>
> Because they met not the children of Israel with
> bread and with water, but hired Balaam against
> them, that he should curse them: howbeit our God
> turned the curse into a blessing.
>
> Now it came to pass, when they had heard the
> law, that they separated from Israel all the mixed
> multitude.
>
> In those days saw I in Judah some treading wine
> presses on the sabbath, and bringing in sheaves,
> and lading asses; as also wine, grapes, and figs, and
> all manner of burdens, which they brought into
> Jerusalem on the sabbath day: and I testified
> against them in the day wherein they sold victuals.
>
> There dwelt men of Tyre also therein, which
> brought fish, and all manner of ware, and sold on
> the sabbath unto the children of Judah, and in
> Jerusalem.
>
> Then I contended with the nobles of Judah, and
> said unto them, What evil thing is this that ye do,
> and profane the sabbath day?

Did not your fathers thus, and did not our God bring all this evil upon us, and upon this city? yet ye bring more wrath upon Israel by profaning the sabbath.

And it came to pass, that when the gates of Jerusalem began to be dark before the sabbath, I commanded that the gates should be shut, and charged that they should not be opened till after the sabbath: and some of my servants set I at the gates, that there should no burden be brought in on the sabbath day.

So the merchants and sellers of all kind of ware lodged without Jerusalem once or twice.

Then I testified against them, and said unto them, Why lodge ye about the wall? if ye do so again, I will lay hands on you. From that time forth came they no more on the sabbath.

And I commanded the Levites that they should cleanse themselves, and that they should come and keep the gates to sanctify the sabbath day. Remember me, O my God, concerning this also, and spare me according to the greatness of thy mercy.

In those days also saw I Jews that had married wives of Ashdod, of Ammon, and of Moab:

And their children spake half in the speech of Ashdod, and could not speak in the Jews' language, but according to the language of each people.

And I contended with them, and cursed them, and smote certain of them, and plucked off their hair, and made them swear by God, saying, Ye shall not give your daughters unto their sons, nor take their daughters unto your sons, or for yourselves.

Did not Solomon king of Israel sin by these things? yet among many nations was there no king like him, who was beloved of his God, and God made him king over all Israel: nevertheless even him did outlandish women cause to sin.

Shall we then hearken unto you to do all this great evil, to transgress against our God in marrying strange wives?

And one of the sons of Joiada, the son of Eliashib
the high priest, was son in law to Sanballat the
Horonite: therefore I chased him from me.
(Neh. 13: 1-3 and 15-28, AV)

Thus, the war of the Maccabees against their Seleucid
masters was not simply a battle between the Jews and the
Syrians but between the orthodox and the hellenists within
the ranks of Judah itself. It was a civil war.

There is no doubt about who won the battle for the soul of
Israel, even allowing for the fact that the victors always get
the better press. The history of Israel in the century before
Christ, and the Israel as represented in the New Testament
documents are sufficient testimony. The spirit of Ezra, that
ready scribe in the law of God, triumphed over the spirit of
Ecclesiastes. The very fact that the picture of his activity is
idealised by the Chronicler bears witness to the fact that he
had already triumphed. The people of Israel henceforth were
to be a people, in Palestine or in the Diaspora, who, in their
rigorous subjection to the Torah as increasingly elaborated by
the scribes, would be found in the ghetto not in the council
chamber, would attend the synagogue school not the academy
down the road, would cultivate the language of Canaan not
the language of the cultivated man of the world. They were to
apply the Law in all its rigours to themselves and their
families. But even this was not enough and the time would
come when the more fervent spirits amongst them would
follow the "teacher of righteousness" to the inhospitable
shores of the Dead Sea, there better to keep the law and to
maintain the faith against the Hellenic spirit. The spirit of
Ezra and Nehemiah broods over the site of Qumran, building
desert walls against the world, driving out apostates and
insisting on meticulous purity of body, mind and spirit. I do
not myself care for the spirit of Ezra and Nehemiah but
honesty compels me to recognise that without them and their
successors Israel would have been lost, as so many other
ethnic groups were lost, in the sea of the surrounding
paganism. Hellenism is a persuasive, attractive ideal but it
manifestly lacks the power to achieve that ideal—and our
modern tyrannies are a witness to that fact. Judaism, for all
its sometimes unlovely fanaticism, has nevertheless survived

as a reminder that we are not free to prescribe our own
objectives or seek our own fulfilment, that each citizen is not
"master of his own person in all circumstances with
exceeding grace and versatility". There are dark forces at
work in the human psyche which constantly give the lie to
that splendid vision. To the Jewish mind the ideal human
existence is submission to the will of God; that submission
was expressed in a variety of ways in the course of Israel's
history—obedience to Moses in the wilderness, membership
of the covenant people, adherence to the anointed king of the
Davidic line, and when all else failed, costly subjection in
detail to the Torah of God received at Sinai.

As a student of the Bible I can only conclude that this is the
way God intends. But although we recognise in the provision
of the Torah that which is for our good, there is a fanatical
devotion to the Torah which carries with it, dare I say,
certain misunderstandings of its purpose. The Jews of the
post-exilic period came to see the law as a mark of national
identity, as a symbol of ethnic solidarity, as a guarantee of
salvation and a means of acquiring merit in God's sight. If
salvation could have been of the law those sectaries of
Qumran ought to have been sure of it. But they had lost sight
of an earlier insight into the meaning of the law which saw it
not as a mighty obstacle to be somehow surmounted but as a
loving provision of our Heavenly Father for our good. At its
best, Rabbinism has always held fast to that truth, but at its
worst it has sadly defaced it. The moral tone of the Jewish
communities of the Diaspora was widely admired, as indeed
it is to this day in the modern Diaspora. It is a great thing
and a costly one to accept the yoke of the law—to worship
God alone, to resist the idols the world creates for us, to
abstain from fornication and stand against the blandishments
of wealth. That is a way of life we Gentiles could well
embrace, thus learning to walk in the way that leads to
Eternal Life. But too often, alas, Judaism, in its brave stand
against Hellenism, sacrificed universality to sectarianism,
sacrificed mercy to fanaticism, sacrificed faith in a loving God
to an unlovely exclusivism. We await now the verdict of two
of Israel's greatest sons upon that Judaism which they
encountered in their own day—Saul of Tarsus and Jesus of
Nazareth.

He crosses the bridges of all the ages
The bridges of all contradictions
From the left bank to the right bank
From yes to no from just to unjust.

Yvan Goll
Jean Sans Terre

IX

Saul of Tarsus

We move now from the Old Testament to the New, although I could wish that the division had never been expressed in this way. Whatever its components from the past the Bible is one book, purporting to deal with the history and beliefs of the Chosen People of God. Judaism understandably regards that book as complete with the closing of the third canon. Everything beyond that comprises commentary, explication, application. Christians, equally understandably, believe in what might preferably be called a fourth canon, i.e. a series of writings continuous with the first three canons and purporting to show that the age-long aspirations of the Jewish people were fulfilled in the coming of Jesus of Nazareth and the re-formation of the People of God, the new Israel. To the Jew the fourth canon is a series of writings from an heretical Jewish sect; to the Christian the first three canons comprise a series of writings which are inexplicable except in the light of what happened in Bethlehem, in Nazareth and in Jerusalem in the first century of the Christian era. But neither Jew nor Christian could deny the closest possible connection between them. Jesus of Nazareth was a Jew, reared in the traditions of His fathers and devoted to their Scriptures. The twelve apostles were, without exception, Jews and were deemed to represent the twelve tribes of the undivided Israel. All the writings of the fourth canon (the New Testament) were by Jews, with the exception of Luke-Acts written by a Gentile who, it is presumed, worshipped the God of Israel in the ranks of the so-called "God-fearers".

When the similarities between the first three and the fourth canons are accepted and their intimate connection with each other is recognised we can afford to observe the undoubted differences between them. The format of the fourth canon is different. It is divided into two distinct parts—the Gospels and the Epistles. Three of the Gospels resemble each other and undoubtedly depend on each other for similarities in content and wording. The fourth is distinct from them and reflects the situation in the Church later than the situation of the first three. The Epistles are precisely what they purport to be—a series of letters, mostly written on the spur of the moment, to deal with precise historical situations which are not always apparent to us. What comprises the unity of the fourth canon is the assumption underlying all the documents that Jesus of Nazareth was not only the Messiah for whom the Jews had been waiting but also the Saviour of the whole inhabited world. But this assumption clearly puts the authors of the Gospels and the Epistles at variance with contemporary Judaism, of which every single one of the authors had been a member. Each one had had to accept a drastic revision of his ancestral faith to make room for an historical personage named Jesus of Nazareth whom they acknowledged as Lord but whose person remained, as to this day, impenetrably mysterious. To put it more plainly, by virtue of what he was saying each author represented in the fourth canon found himself at odds with his fellow Jews on the most fundamental tenet of his faith and of theirs. To him Jesus was the true Messiah. To them He was a false Messiah. As great a gulf separated them as separated Dives from Lazarus. To a greater extent therefore than in any other extant literature of the Hebrew people, the fourth canon arose out of controversy—and that controversy is to be found everywhere in it. It is more obvious, of course, in the Epistles where Paul explicitly argues with representatives of his own people in an attempt to justify his faith and practice. It is less obvious to the casual reader of the Gospels that the Gospels too arose from and reflect controversy. We shall need to remember that the authors of two of the Gospels were at one time and another companions of Paul, and it would be unlikely that they could have written without a painful awareness of Paul's controversy with the Jews. The so-called conflict stories of St. Mark are not just transcripts of the conflicts in which our Lord Himself was involved; they reflect and indeed point out precisely the same conflicts regarding sabbath observance, relationships with aliens and dietary rules, which Paul and Luke and Mark experienced in their journeys round the synagogues of the near Middle East and Europe. In Matthew the controversy is even more sharply expressed in a series of "woes" upon the Scribes and Pharisees. The fourth canon has to be read this way if we are to be true to the intention of the authors; we have to learn to distinguish between utterances which arise out of a particular situation and relate to a controversial matter of local and topical importance from those utterances which are the essence of the faith and, although arising out of a temporary controversy, have a permanent significance in the life and thought of the Church. The fourth canon is almost entirely for Jews or about Jews. We have to bear this solitary but important fact in mind as we begin to address ourselves to the subject of this chapter, Saul of Tarsus, himself the author of a substantial part of the writings which comprise the fourth canon.

The second factor regarding the fourth canon which we have to bear in mind—and a factor which distinguishes the fourth canon from the other three—is that it arose out of, and served as, an aid to mission. The only comparable document in the Old Testament which has this as its subject is the Book of Jonah. St. Mark has sometimes been called, probably with some truth, a handbook for the Christian preacher. Certainly parts of St. Matthew provide material for the instruction of Jews converted to the Christian faith. St. Luke's work, Luke-Acts, is all of a piece. His Gospel arises out of the missionary experience in which he was involved personally and which is reflected in the Acts of the Apostles. St. John has everywhere mission in mind—the mission to the Samaritans symbolised, for example, in our Lord's conversation with a Samaritan woman, and the mission to the Gentiles reflected in the account of our Lord's encounter with the Greeks. Paul's letters have invariably as their subject an aspect of Christ's mission to the Jews and to the world and the consequences of that mission for faith and conduct. They are the letters of a missionary as well as of a controversialist. They are not concerned just with the truth as it is in Christ, but with the implications of that truth for Paul's own people, the Jews, and for the people whom he evangelised, the Gentiles. The writings of the New Testament, therefore, do not comprise and certainly do not aim at a cool assessment of the life and teaching of Jesus of Nazareth, nor do they contemplate for themselves a permanent place in the religious history of the world. It was to be three centuries before the writings of the Apostles came to be associated with the writings of the Old Testament and to be given equal authority with them. Matthew, Mark, Luke, John, Paul, Peter and James were not writing Holy Scripture. They found themselves in a situation of heated controversy and no little physical danger because they insisted on treating the coming of Christ as a missionary matter. No one would have bothered them much if they had been content to remain as representatives of a breakaway sect of Judaism. Judaism was full of sects in the time of our Lord. Those early believers in Jesus could no doubt have procured for themselves an uncomfortable but peaceful site on the shores of the Dead Sea where they could have cultivated their faith and developed their cult quite untroubled by controversy or physical danger. What marked the Christian sect off from all other sects within Judaism was its conviction that their faith was the faith for all the Jews and, what is more, for all mankind. The New Testament is a testimony to that conviction and must be read in that way.

With these, I believe necessary, qualifications in our minds we can now turn to the main subject of this chapter which is—Saul of Tarsus. I shall be concerned with only one aspect of his life and his theology (which are, as we shall see, inextricably associated with each other)—and that is his attitude to the law. I hardly need to say that this is crucial to the understanding of the matter we have in hand. If we are to maintain the view that the Torah of God has permanent significance for the life of the world we shall have to be convinced that Paul's attitude does not give it the lie. After all he was a Jew, a Hebrew of the Hebrews, a Pharisee of the Pharisees, and the only Rabbi whose writings figure in the New Testament. The prevailing impression made on the mind, in the first instance, by a reading of the letters is that we are in the presence of a man who has abolished the law in favour of the Gospel, has abolished divine enactments in favour of the spirit and has abolished Moses in favour of the Christ. This is certainly what many Christians believe and what many Jews believe we believe. Is it true? If it is, then I have been wasting my time and yours; you will have been subjected to an academic exercise which maybe has sown some useful seeds in your mind, but which is of dubious theological value in its main thrust and painfully irrelevant to the issues which I feel are crucial for a right understanding of society and for a correct assessment of the relationship between freedom and law. I could still be right in my main contention, but I would have to forfeit any reliance upon Holy Scripture. May I say to the reader that I have had my moments, largely produced by the studies I have conducted in preparation for this book, when I have doubted the thesis. By now, however, I have reached a certain solid ground and doubts are behind me—although as always they cannot be replaced as we would like by certainties. What then are we to say of Paul as he struggles with an issue infinitely painful for himself and subsequently painful for the world? What part, if any, does the law, represented by the Sinai experience, play in his vision of the future? As we begin to look for an answer it will be necessary to bear in mind that Paul's "future" was for the greater part of his life short. He continued to believe, with the majority of his fellow believers, that the Messiah would return within the lifetime of the last of the Apostles. Some say that his theology *matured* to take account of a larger perspective. To that we can only rejoin that his theology certainly *grew up* under the influence of the expectation of the end of the world. St. Paul was not legislating for a remote future, nor could he have expected that his casual, off-the-cuff letters would become the subject of bitter acrimony amongst theologians and the cause of bitter and permanent divisions in the Church. He wrote indeed out of the fullness of his understanding, but was not always conscious of the emotions which moved him or the intellectual impulses which helped to form his mind. He was a missionary with a burning zeal for communicating the truth of Christ to the world and a pastoral concern for those primitive Christian communities he had had a hand in creating.

But before he became a missionary he was a Rabbi in Tarsus. One of the ironies of the situation is that whilst his life is, at some stages, the most fully documented in the Bible, we in fact know almost nothing about the early stages of his life, about his family, his upbringing or even his professional activities before we find him stunned and blind on the road to

Damascus. There is a sense in which, from our point of view, he was born on the road to Damascus, not just born again. Like our Lord he had his hidden years but we do not even have the benefit in his case of a family and domestic scenario, such as the birth narratives provide for our Lord. We know he had a sister, we know he had a nephew, we know he was educated in Jerusalem at the feet of Gamaliel and that he belonged to the renewal movement in Israel, known as the Pharisees. We know that he was implicated—and felt implicated—in the execution of Stephen. Arguments can still be heard as to whether he was ever married or not. But we do know that he came from Tarsus and we have some reliable sources of information about Tarsus, about its population, its political status and its dominant cultural patterns.

The most obvious thing to say about Tarsus is that it was not in Palestine. It was some three hundred miles by sea north of Caesarea in the region of Cilicia. It was on the banks of the river Cnydus some ten miles from the coast. It had been, for a time, the western capital of the Assyrian empire and is mentioned in the Black Obelisk as one of the cities captured by Shalmaneser in the ninth century B.C. In origin, therefore, and for a large part of its history it was an oriental town and this aspect of it never entirely disappeared even under the influence of Hellenisation and even when it moved into the orbit of Rome rather than of Persia. Like every other city of the day it was of mixed population and perhaps more than most cities of the day a meeting place of Greeks and orientals. It was one of the great university cities of the Mediterranean world vying with Athens and Alexandria for supremacy. It was a centre of Greek intellectual life, boasting the name of Nestor as one of the great philosophers of Paul's time. It was the capital city of the region. Paul then was a Diaspora Jew, confronting precisely the problems that were described in the previous chapter. The fact that his father chose for him a higher education in Jerusalem at the feet of Gamaliel, in preference to the attractive intellectual facilities of Tarsus, suggests that he came of an Orthodox family, attracted no doubt, but not captured by, the all-pervading Hellenism. But the fact that Paul was by his own admission a Roman citizen, and moreover born free, suggests that his family was one of some substance, which played a part in civic and political life. They were not ashamed to name themselves citizens of Rome, whatever their attitude may have been to the religion of Rome. The questions to which we now turn have exercised the minds of Jewish and Christian scholars for a century and more, and they are these. To what extent, and in what ways was Paul's attitude to the law formed by his environment? Is he the intellectual product of Jerusalem or of Tarsus, of Palestinian Judaism or the Diaspora? Is he representative at all of the Judaism of his day, or did his experience on the road to Damascus fuse with a white heat his intellectual structures into an altogether different shape, incapable of being attributed to Palestine or to the Diaspora, but only to a sovereign intervention by the risen Christ?

It is not to be supposed that there are any easy answers to these questions. There seldom are. If there were, scholars would no longer be writing long books about them. Churches would no longer be disagreeing with each other about them, and social philosophers would more readily apply themselves to the issues of freedom and law in society on the basis of the certain rather than conjectural. So on this one issue alone in the theology of St. Paul book follows book with unfailing regularity. In 1948, W. D. Davies wrote a book which has been on the reading list for theological students ever since, entitled *Paul and Rabbinic Judaism—Some Rabbinic Elements in Pauline Theology.* He is concerned, as his publisher says, with

> ... demonstrating that despite the Hellenistic elements in his thought, Paul of Tarsus stood within the main current of first-century Rabbinic Judaism, and is best understood as a Pharisee, who had come to accept Jesus of Nazareth as the Messiah. The Apostle remained, as far as was possible, a practising Jew who agonized over his people, and never lost his sense of oneness with the "Old Israel", whilst in his theology it was to Rabbinic concepts that he chiefly turned in his wrestling to interpret Christ and the Christian life. Pauline Christianity, it is contended, is not the

antithesis of Rabbinic Judaism but its fulfilment "in Christ".

His conclusion is that,

> ... for the Apostle the Christian Faith was the full flowering of Judaism, the outcome of the latter and its fulfilment; in being obedient to the Gospel he was merely being obedient to the true form of Judaism. The Gospel for Paul was not the annulling of Judaism but its completion, and as such it took up into itself the essential genius of Judaism.
>
> This latter fact came out most clearly when we dealt with the concept of the Torah and of obedience in relation to Paul's thought. Lev Gillet has recently written: "The religion of Paul became centred on a person, Jesus himself. This personality could by no means be expressed in terms of Torah." But, if our thesis be correct, this is exactly what we do find in Paul, the application to the Person of Jesus of those concepts which Judaism had reserved for its greatest treasure, the Torah, so that we felt justified in describing the Pauline Christ as a New Torah. We found in Paul a "Christifying" of the Torah and ipso facto a "spiritualizing" of it. This last, however, does not mean that the concept correlative to that of the Torah in Judaism, namely, obedience, is absent from the Gospel of Paul; indeed, we saw that it was central to it. Paul was the preacher of a New Exodus wrought by the "merit" of Christ who was obedient unto death, but this New Exodus like the Old was constitutive of community, it served to establish the New Israel; it also led to the foot of a New Sinai, and Paul appeared before us as a catechist, the steward of a New Didache that imposed new demands. "Torah", "Obedience" and "Community" then are integral to Pauline Christianity no less than to Judaism.

In 1961, H. J. Schoeps wrote a book entitled *Paul—The Theology of the Apostle in the Light of Jewish Religious History*. "It is our conviction", he says "that Judaistic Hellenism represents an essential factor which is to be taken note of for the reconstruction of the doctrine and faith of Saul the Diaspora Pharisee." The core of his argument as it relates to Paul's attitude to the law is suggested by the heading of Section 6 of Chapter 5—"Paul's Fundamental Misapprehension". The misapprehension is that "Paul succumbed to a characteristic distortion of vision which had its antecedents in the spiritual outlook of Judaic Hellenism. Paul did not perceive, and for various reasons was perhaps unable to perceive, that in the biblical view the law is integral to the covenant; in modern terms was the constitutive act by which the Sinai covenant was ratified, the basic ordinance which God laid down for His 'house of Israel'." In 1977, E. P. Sanders wrote what reviewers described as a "magisterial" treatment of the subject entitled *Paul and Palestinian Judaism—A Comparison of Patterns of Religion*. His conclusion, which is at variance both with Dr. Davies and with Dr. Schoeps, is that,

> We cannot give an account here of Paul's relationship to all the contemporary religious movements, but it does appear that it may be just as difficult to peg him as a Hellenistic Jew who thought that Christ presented the true mystery or true gnosis as it is to characterise him as a Rabbinic Jew who thought that Jesus was the Messiah. In his letters Paul appears as one who bases the explanations of his gospel, his theology, on the meaning of the death and resurrection of Jesus, not as one who has fitted the death and resurrection into a pre-existing scheme, where they take the place of other motifs with similar functions.

On a matter therefore which is basic to our understanding of Paul's attitude to the law, which cannot but have been partly determined by the Judaism of his day, we find three distinguished authors, specialists in their field, disagreeing radically with each other—and each of them armed with arguments well substantiated from the literature of Paul's time. Have we any resource for making our own judgment on a matter which, as Christians, Jews or just as citizens, concerns us all deeply? Is the Jew to believe that his ancestral faith, inextricably bound up with the law of Moses given at Sinai, was somehow mistaken, and that Saul of Tarsus was the first to get it right? Is the Christian to believe that we have no authoritative guidance from Saul of Tarsus about the nature of liberty and law in the Church and in his own personal life? And does the citizen have no appeal from blatant totalitarianism on the one hand and vague liberalism on the other, to some well-tried accessible source of knowledge. On a matter which is crucial to the health and even to the survival of society, do we find ourselves on our own? At some stage I hope to be reassuring, but first of all we shall need to consult the testimony of Scripture itself, as distinct from a discussion of the milieu out of which that Scripture arose. Paul's Epistles are, after all, part of Holy Writ regardless of the influences which may or may not have influenced him, whether he was a Palestinian Rabbi or a Diaspora Rabbi. Surely we do not need to be clear about his pedigree before we can assert the validity and authority which he undoubtedly possesses as a chosen Apostle of Christ and a leader in the early Church. There are indeed certain things which are crystal clear in his presentation of the faith. He speaks unambiguously of the Lordship and the finality of Christ. It is clear to him that what he believed as a result of his experience of salvation through Christ was available to all, Jew and Gentile alike. He looked forward with unfailing hope to the triumph of Christ over all men, over all the earth and throughout the whole cosmos. Alas, however, he is not unambiguous in his treatment of the matter before us, this for reasons which will be obvious when I mention them. His letters were not cool dissertations written for pupils or fellow academics—and Paul would surely have been astonished to find them treated so. He does not cross every "t" or dot every "i". He does not guard against every possible misapprehension. He does not always choose his words carefully and he does not have in view the status which was later conferred on him as a writer of Holy Scripture. He was writing always under pressure and nearly always with a quite specific issue in mind. As we have seen, the Epistles are the product of mission and controversy. Furthermore, they are addressed to recipients, sometimes individual, sometimes corporate, whose problems are different and whose assumptions are unknowable. The Galatians were not Corinthians, the Romans were not Colossians. It is impossible to identify with any precision exactly what the controversy was, or what his opponents exactly believed. If you doubt that, I invite you to study John Drane's recent book *Paul—Libertine or Legalist?* and observe some of his chapter headings, e.g. "Who were Paul's Opponents—in Galatia and Corinth?", "How Gnostic is Galatians?", "Were Paul's Opponents Gnostics?" I do not expect you to answer those questions; they probably require more detailed knowledge than most of us possess. I just ask you to believe that there are problems which simple attention to the text will never solve. On the face of it it is extremely unlikely that the systematic view of the relationships between the Jew and the Christian believer could ever emerge from a correspondence so varied and so casual. I tremble to think what a subsequent reader of some of my own letters would deduce from them. Today it is a letter to a retired Army officer in Eastbourne about law and order. The day before yesterday it was a letter to the secretary of a Parochial Church Council in Yorkshire about the effects of the charismatic movement in his parish. Tomorrow it could be a letter to the Minister of State about freedom of choice on an educational matter in Liverpool. The day after tomorrow it could be a disagreeable case of clergy discipline where the law has to be invoked. But just suppose that this unhappy reader of my letters had no idea to whom they were addressed, no knowledge of twentieth-century society and no means of discovering whether I was writing as a parish priest, the head of a theological college, the Bishop of Liverpool or the Archbishop of York. And suppose he knew next to nothing about my own social or intellectual background. If that is not enough to deter any would-be dogmatist, may I allude to another difficulty. It is reasonable to suppose that Paul's views may have changed, or even developed. The arguments on this matter have been a matter of scholarly debate for a century and more and Dr. Drane still has to write a chapter entitled—"How did Paul's Theology Develop?". It is true, of

course, that he had been a Christian a long time before he
began writing letters about it and that his letter-writing stage
lasted for little more than fifteen years. Nevertheless there are
clear evidences of adjustment to changing situations even
within the letters themselves. Like many another Christian he
had to come to terms with the fact that our Lord did not
return in glory within the lifetime of the Apostles, as the
Church almost universally believed; there is a noticeable
change of emphasis between the letter to the Thessalonians
and the letter to the Romans. There is evidence of an
enlargement of his view of redemption to include a panoramic
view of the salvation, not only of the Jews and the Gentiles,
but of all mankind and of the whole cosmos. But the issue
which tested him more sharply than any was the issue
regarding the law and its authority over Christians. It was
this controversy which threatened his relationship with the
other Apostles (he violently disagreed with Peter) and could
easily have divided the Church irreparably. It was at this
point that he was constantly challenged by Gentiles and Jews
alike—by Gentiles who valued their freedom and proceeded
to make use of it, sometimes in extravagent ways; by Jews
who perceived that contempt for the Torah brought in its
train unimaginable horrors. It was not only Paul who had to
choose between being a "Libertine" and a "Legalist". In this
matter, change or development is surely inevitable. Paul
stands for liberty, and seemingly creates licence. He rebukes
licence and seemingly enthrones the law. He is not, and never
could be, under his circumstances, a systematic theologian,
but he may well remain, inwardly at least, a consistent
theologian.

> In taking the position that Paul was a coherent, but
> not systematic, thinker, we are taking the position
> most common among exegetes, and it needs little
> defence. That Paul was a thinker is readily seen in
> the way he tried to work out solutions to problems
> by re-thinking the Christian tradition. This can be
> seen most clearly in the Corinthian correspondence,
> where Paul dealt with a succession of problems. He
> never simply answers with a formula or with a
> biblical quotation, although he makes use of both.

Both are re-thought and applied to the particular
question in what is probably a unique way.
                    Sanders—*Paul and Palestinian Judaism*

I shall have to add a further cautionary note—there remains
still considerable disagreement about when the letters were
written, and in what order. Development or change, therefore, which we must I think assume, cannot be convincingly
associated with particular letters in a nice straight line. We
cannot automatically claim greater authority for the later
letters than for the earlier ones.

I hope I have by now reduced the reader to despair, if only
to condition him to the possibility of another, and I believe
more fruitful, approach. My starting point is an important
judgment made by Dr. Sanders on page 496,

> What is distinctive about Paul's view of the law—
> and in fact about his theology—was correctly
> pointed to in the statement quoted from Davies:
> Christ saves Gentiles as well as Jews. This was not
> only a theological view, but it was bound up with
> Paul's most profound conviction about himself, a
> conviction on which he staked his career and his
> life: he was the apostle to the Gentiles. The sal-
> vation of the Gentiles is essential to Paul's
> preaching; and with it falls the law; for, as Paul
> says simply, Gentiles cannot live by the law.

Whatever else may be wrong, that surely must be right.
Paul's life was changed by a staggering experience of One
whom he perceived to be the risen Christ. It was a typical
prophetic experience, not unlike that of an Isaiah or a
Jeremiah or an Amos, containing within it a distinct and
wholly unexpected demand, to which the prophets almost
invariably answered with some such words as "woe is me".
Paul's "woe" began on the Damascus road. He, a Pharisee of
the Pharisees and a rabbi, had been heavily conditioned by
the belief that the Hebrews were God's chosen people.
Salvation was of the Jews. To him the Gentiles were unclean.
He is now being commanded to go to the Gentiles and take
the news of Christ to them on equal terms with the Jews.

This is not quite as unprecedented as we might suppose. After all, Jesus Himself acknowledged that the Pharisees were zealous evangelists—they compassed heaven and earth to make a single proselyte. But all the evidence from the ancient world is that the Pharisees were not conspicuously successful and it is not difficult to see why. They insisted that their converts should keep the law in all its rigour as the price of their being numbered amongst the people of God. Judaism may indeed have been occasionally aware of a worldwide mission, but the conditions that were habitually imposed virtually excluded the possibility of success. Whatever Paul's attitude to the law may have been before, or immediately after his conversion, there was no significant way he could "go to the Gentiles" if, in agreement with his previous practice as a Pharisee, he had insisted on obedience to the law. Any Gentile who attempted such was virtually condemning himself to the ghetto, whether it was a big ghetto in Alexandria or a small ghetto in Corinth. To insist on obedience to the law, therefore, would be to exclude the possibility of salvation through Christ. At that point, decision was inescapable and Paul made it in a way which determined whether the Christian faith would remain a sect of Judaism or a worldwide religion. So, with the Galatians he is quite clear that those who were insisting on the obedience to the law were controverting the Gospel and destroying the Church, and were compromising their new-found liberty in Christ. The law was not and never could be a means of universal salvation and to insist on it would have made Paul's vision on the road to Damascus meaningless. Whatever else he may have sometimes doubted, he never doubted Christ's call to be the apostle to the Gentiles. But of course, in the process of an argument, he could not rest on that experience alone; he had in some measure to rationalise, to argue, to demonstrate, on the basis of the Scriptures that both he and his Jewish opponents had received. Hence the often tortuous arguments which seem strangely unconvincing to us about the role of the law in the life of Israel and its relationship with the Christ event. It was a tutor to bring us to Christ or an interim measure, or a painful reminder of our inadequacy, or a loving concession of God to our weakness. But like many another initiator of a powerful spiritual movement, Paul had to learn the lesson that not all his followers were possessed of the balancing mechanism in his own mind, nor did they share in his moral and spiritual inheritance. The "liberty in Christ" meant something a little different to the Galatians and the Corinthians, and Paul had to learn how different it could be. By the time he was writing his Epistle to the Romans (and there is no doubt that that Epistle is subsequent to the Epistle to the Galatians) he is expressing himself in a different way. The law is holy and good. Christ came that "the just requirements of the law might be fulfilled in us who walk not according to the flesh but according to the spirit" so I can hardly do better at this point than to quote from Dr. Drane's book,

> Was Paul a libertine or a legalist? What has been said already in this study will provide the answer. He was at heart neither. He was simply "a man in Christ" (2 Cor. 12: 2), whose main aim in life was to serve the One who had so radically affected his life on the Damascus road. From that day on, Paul was convinced that the end-product of Christian faith was the production of a life that was Christlike. In his encounter with the Galatian Judaisers, as with the Gnosticisers of Corinth, that was his main ambition. They were all "my little children, with whom I am ... in travail until Christ be formed in you" (Gal. 4: 19). In his enthusiasm for his vocation Paul made many blunders, as we would expect from even the best of men. He wrote many things that could be construed as either antinomian or legalistic, things which, on later reflection, he may have expressed quite differently, or not have expressed at all. But through all his problems, he had the same goal before him to the end of his life, "that I may gain Christ, and be found in him, not having a righteousness of my own, based on law, but that which is through faith in Christ, the righteousness of God ..." (Phil. 3: 9). If the gaining of divine righteousness meant that he needed to be at times either a libertine to win back the Judaisers, or a

legalist to restore would-be Gnostics, that was a
risk he was prepared to take: "I do it all for the
sake of the gospel, that I may share in its
blessings." (1 Cor. 9: 23)

My conclusion is that there is nothing in Paul's writings,
understood in this way, to forbid that the Torah should be
regarded as a legitimate guide to human beings, Jew and
Gentile, in the way of life. What is absolutely clear for St.
Paul is that observance of the law was never intended as, and
never could be, a means of salvation. Salvation in his view
was a sheer gift of God, through Christ, to those who believed
in Him. In that sense, and in that sense alone, Christ was the
"end" of the "law". But Christ was not the "end" of the law
in the sense that we could now dispense with it altogether.
That law is holy and good and a gift of God to mankind for
the guiding of personal conduct and the ordering of social life.
Am I entitled, in my liberty in Christ, to neglect my parents,
to worship images, to commit adultery, to murder, to bear
false witness, to steal and to covet? The answer must be no.
And why?—because these things are forbidden in a law of
God revealed at Sinai which remains the law of God for all
mankind. What advantage do I have then over the Jew? The
only advantage that Saul of Tarsus, himself a Jew, was able
to claim—that he now had within him a capacity to observe
and to rejoice in that law which was previously utterly
beyond his reach. Christians and Jews therefore stand
together in their belief that the law was holy and good and
was intended for all mankind. We divide at the point at
which the orthodox Jew seeks to fulfil that law by minute
adherence to the letter of the law and the Christian seeks to
fulfil it by faith in Christ and obedience to the spirit of the
law. We shall have to discuss in the next chapter whether this
view of the matter accords with what we understand to be the
teaching of Paul's older contemporary, Jesus of Nazareth.

If the Son of Man shall set you free, you shall be free indeed.

St. John

It is not revolutions and upheavals
That clear the road to new and better days,
But revelations, lavishness and torments
Of someone's soul, inspired and ablaze.

Boris Pasternak
After the Storm; trans. Lydia Pasternak Slater; from
Fifty Poems

X

Jesus of Nazareth

Let a man of his own race have the first word. I quote from Martin Buber, one of the great Jewish theologians of this century, in his book *Two Types of Faith* :

> From my youth onwards I have found in Jesus my great brother. That Christianity has regarded and does regard him as God and Saviour has always appeared to me a fact of the highest importance which, for his sake and my own, I must endeavor to understand ... My own fraternally open relationship to him has grown ever stronger and clearer, and today (1950) I see him more strongly and clearly than ever before.
>
> I am more than ever certain that a great place belongs to him in Israel's history of faith and that this place cannot be described by any of the usual categories.

Whatever may be one's attitude to the dogmatic structures erected upon the life and teaching of Jesus of Nazareth, no one will dispute His prime importance in the history of the world. He cannot be described "by any of the normal categories". More even than Saul of Tarsus, therefore, He bears responsibility for the particular view of the place of law in human society and in the life of the individual. It may not have been easy to distinguish between the less authoritative and the more authoritative of Paul's writings. But now we are in the presence of one who in terms of history and theology towers over prophet, priest, wise man and apostle. He fills the earth. But we must not exaggerate the differences between Paul and Jesus. Powerful voices in the world of scholarship have been raised to attribute to Paul rather than to Jesus prime responsibility for the intellectual and spiritual

structures of the Church. The simple faith of Jesus has been
corrupted by the dogmatisms of Paul—crudely put, that is
how the argument has sometimes gone. On the surface indeed
the differences between the two men are striking. Paul was a
Rabbi of the traditional school, and a pedant. Jesus was
ridiculed by His opponents as an unlearned man. Paul was a
member of the Greek Diaspora and a Roman citizen. Jesus
was a Palestinian who seldom moved outside the borders of
Israel and spent the greater part of His life in an unattractive
and, even by Palestinian standards, an unpretentious town.
"Can any good come out of Nazareth?" Nathaniel said.
Paul's attitude towards women was at best typical of his day.
Jesus, to an extent unusual in His day, made room in His
company for women disciples. Paul's method of teaching
remained until the end of his days typical of the Rabbinic
schools, with attachment to precise interpretation of the
written word. Jesus' exact quotations from Scripture are
relatively few and His teaching was marked by a certain
freedom and humour which made a deep impression on His
hearers. He teaches, they said, with authority and not as the
Scribes. Paul disdains, or is perhaps incapable of using
domestic or rural illustrations. Jesus relied upon such
illustrations for the delineation of truth in such a way as to
make it comprehensible to ordinary people who, the
Evangelist says, heard Him gladly. Paul wrote powerful
letters but by his own admission was not impressive in public.
Jesus wrote nothing but thousands flocked to hear Him.

The contrasts may thus be plainly stated but they may
easily mask the equally striking similarities between the two
men. To begin with, the contrast between life in the Diaspora
and life in the homeland may not be as obvious as we might
suppose. In the last chapter we found that learned scholars
familiar with the material disagreed with each other for
example on the extent to which Paul was indebted on the one
hand to Diaspora Hellenism and on the other to Palestinian
Judaism. Earlier in this book we have been made aware of an
all-pervading Hellenism, which was as active in Israel as
outside it. Jesus of Nazareth and Saul of Tarsus may indeed
have lived three hundred miles away from each other but both
were part of a common culture and subjects of the one
Imperial Rome. To Pontius Pilate, to Festus, to Felix and to

many another Roman Governor, the only difference between
Palestine and Cilicia was the violence by which the
Palestinians served their inexplicable causes and pursued
their own mysterious aims. Jesus and Paul belonged alike to
the Oicumene. In other respects also their lives had certain
similarities. They both found themselves in conflict with the
guardians of the law and the leaders of their people. Both
stood before the High Priest, the one silent, the other
vituperative. Paul called the High Priest a "whited wall".
Both of them were brought before kings and governors at the
instigation of their own countrymen. Both of them broke with
the sacred traditions of their people. Paul companied with
Gentiles, Jesus accepted the friendship of publicans and
sinners and even went out of His way to commend the
Samaritans and to heal Greeks. And, to come to our main
point, both were radical interpreters of the law. Saul was
driven to his position by his irresistible calling to preach to
the Gentiles which, to be in any sense effective, had to come
to terms with the fact that the Gentiles could not keep the
Jewish law. Jesus was driven to His position by the plain
observation that there were those within the ranks of Israel
itself who, by virtue of their occupation, could never keep the
law as the lawyers prescribed it. Paul had to resist the
demands of his fellow Rabbis in the interests of his mission to
the Gentiles. Jesus had to resist the demands of the Rabbis in
the interests of His mission to the disaffected, the alienated,
the despised amongst His own people. It is a mistake to
suppose that the Jews of Palestine were all loyal worshipping
members of the synagogue. As in many a so-called Christian
nation today, the synagogue was the place they stayed away
from. Not all children of Abraham were welcome in the
synagogues of Israel. Like Paul after him, Jesus began His
ministry in a synagogue at Nazareth, but found Himself
compelled to do the bulk of His teaching in the open air,
where publicans and sinners, the lepers and the insane, could
come to Him without restriction. For both Jesus and Paul it
was the unexpected response of those who, for whatever
reason, stood outside the law that made them radical interpreters of it. It could not have been otherwise if Jesus was to
speak to the despised "people of the land" or Paul to the
despised "Gentile dogs". But the circumstances were different

in each case. The teacher of disaffected Jews would be likely to use models rather different from those employed by a teacher to the Gentiles.

With these similarities and contrasts in mind, we now turn to what is represented to us in the Gospels as the teaching of Christ regarding the law. It is perhaps necessary to say that Jesus must be regarded as a "teacher of the law". Although never formally trained as such He is called Rabbi (or Lord), He wore (as some commentators still believe) the official "hem" regarded as the sartorial sign of the Rabbi. "You call me Lord, Lord (Rabbi, Rabbi) and so I am," He said. He "taught", so the evangelists tell us, using the Greek equivalent for the Hebrew word which invariably means to "teach the law". He quoted freely from the Decalogue in His initial response to the young man who came to Him for guidance.

> As he was starting out on a journey, a stranger ran up, and, kneeling before him, asked, "Good Master, what must I do to win eternal life?" Jesus said to him, "Why do you call me good? No one is good except God alone. You know the commandments: 'Do not murder; do not commit adultery; do not steal; do not give false evidence; do not defraud; honour your father and mother.'" "But, Master," he replied, "I have kept all these since I was a boy." Jesus looked straight at him; his heart warmed to him, and he said, "One thing you lack: go, sell everything you have, and give to the poor, and you will have riches in heaven; and come, follow me." At these words his face fell and he went away with a heavy heart; for he was a man of great wealth. (Mark 10: 17-22)

It is not as fanciful as it may sound to suggest that the whole of the so-called Sermon on the Mount could have been an extended commentary on the law. Certainly St. Matthew wished us to understand, by placing the Sermon on the Mount rather than on the plain as in St. Luke, that the people of Israel were in the presence of a new Sinai, a new Moses and a new Torah. If His teaching had not been concerned with the law and therefore a challenge to the authorised teachers of the law, He would not have aroused the bitter opposition which is described in all four Gospels. It follows that to attend to His teaching without constant reference to the law which stood behind it is to be sure of misunderstanding it. Behind the little mountain of Galilee where Jesus taught His disciples stands the great mountain of Sinai, still wreathed in smoke and dispensing thunders.

But when we try to identify a positive attitude to the law, suggested by the utterances of Jesus, we find ourselves in much the same uneasy position as we were in trying to identify Paul's attitude to the law. On the one hand, Jesus seems to speak in a cavalier way of His great predecessor Moses:

> On leaving those parts he came into the regions of Judaea and Transjordan; and when a crowd gathered round him once again, he followed his usual practice and taught them. The question was put to him: "Is it lawful for a man to divorce his wife?" This was to test him. He asked in return, "What did Moses command you?" They answered, "Moses permitted a man to divorce his wife by note of dismissal." Jesus said to them, "It was because your minds were closed that he made this rule for you; but in the beginning, at the creation, God made them male and female. For this reason a man shall leave his father and mother, and be made one with his wife; and the two shall become one flesh. It follows that they are no longer two individuals: they are one flesh. What God has joined together, man must not separate." (Mark 10: 1-9)

All the evangelists make the same point in a different way at the end of the transfiguration narrative, when they emphasise the fact that when Moses and Elijah, representing the law and the prophets, had disappeared from the Mount they saw "Jesus only". St. John makes the same point even more harshly when he says: "The law was given by Moses, grace and truth came by Jesus Christ." Yet on the other hand, He is heard to speak with warm devotion of the permanence and finality of the law of Moses.

> Do not suppose that I have come to abolish the Law and the prophets; I did not come to abolish, but to complete. I tell you this: so long as heaven and earth endure, not a letter, not a stroke, will disappear from the Law until all that must happen has happened. If any man therefore sets aside even the least of the Law's demands, and teaches others to do the same, he will have the lowest place in the kingdom of Heaven, whereas anyone who keeps the Law, and teaches others so, will stand high in the kingdom of Heaven. I tell you, unless you show yourselves far better men than the Pharisees and the doctors of the law, you can never enter the kingdom of Heaven. (Matt. 5: 17-20)

If we are to say that there is a law of God given "by revelation to the Chosen People" which is normative for all times, all cultures, all places, then the seeming ambivalence in Jesus' attitude to the law is an embarrassment to us. Is there any way, therefore, of arriving at a cogent and consistent view of Jesus' attitude not simply to the law as His people had received it, but to the whole concept of law as an ingredient of all human society? I turn to this question now with some trepidation, treading as delicately as I can in an academic minefield in which many able scholars of the New Testament have been blown to pieces.

First let me attend to the difficulties of arriving at an accurate record of what Jesus actually said. It is possible that Jesus was familiar with the Greek language; some familiarity with it was almost essential for anyone who carried on a business in the ancient world. But it seems almost indisputable that He conducted His teaching, for the greater part, in Aramaic, a co-lateral descendant of the Hebrew. I quote from Professor Black's invaluable book *An Aramaic Approach to the Gospels and Acts.*

> Four languages were to be found in first-century Palestine: Greek was the speech of the educated

"hellenized" classes and the medium of cultural and commercial intercourse between Jew and foreigner; Latin was the language of the army of occupation and, to judge from Latin borrowings in Aramaic, appears also to some extent to have served the purposes of commerce, as it no doubt also did of Roman law; Hebrew, the sacred tongue of the Jewish Scriptures, continued to provide the lettered Jew with an important means of literary expression and was cultivated as a spoken tongue in the learned coteries of the Rabbis; Aramaic was the language of the people of the land and, together with Hebrew, provided the chief literary medium of the Palestinian Jew of the first century; Josephus wrote his "Jewish War" in Aramaic and later translated it into Greek.

If Jesus was a Galilean Rabbi, it is not unlikely that He made use of Hebrew as well as Aramaic, especially, as T. W. Manson has suggested, in His formal disputations with the Pharisees. M. H. Segal has gone so far as to claim that "Mishnaic" Hebrew, the kind of Hebrew we find in the Mishnah, was actually a spoken vernacular in Judea in the time of Christ. In the Palestinian Talmud Aramaic and Hebrew are found together, sometimes in the form of a kind of "Mischsprache"; sentences half Hebrew, half Aramaic, are familiar to the reader of the Talmud, and this artificial language, rabbinical in origin, may well have been in use before as after the Fall of Jerusalem.

The Gospels were written in a predominantly hellenistic environment, and they were written in Greek. But Greek was not the native language of their central Figure, nor of the earliest apostles, if it was not unfamiliar to them. Jesus must have conversed in the Galilean dialect of Aramaic, and His teaching was probably almost entirely in Aramaic. At the basis of the Greek Gospels, therefore, must lie a Palestinian Aramaic tradition, at any rate of the sayings and teaching of Jesus, and

this tradition must at one time have been translated
from Aramaic into Greek.

The translation from Aramaic or Hebrew to Greek itself
creates problems. To take an example, the word for law in
Greek (nomos) is used variously of the Pentateuch, of the Old
Testament as a whole, of the Decalogue, of the will of God.
The word is used eight times in St. Matthew and nine in St.
Luke, thirteen in St. John, and it is a fruitful source of
misunderstanding. Furthermore, it is likely that the particular emphasis which Jesus gives to the law will vary
somewhat with the audience. To the guardians of the law He
will expose the hollowness of their pretensions and the
ambiguity of the law they profess to teach. To the people of
the land, however, He is more likely to speak of the law, once
delivered from the trammels of an unbending tradition, as
"holy and good". To His disciples He will speak in particular
terms, mindful of the ultimate responsibility of the apostles as
teachers of the new Israel. As in Paul's letters, the immediate
thrust of Jesus' teaching will depend upon whether the
audience is composed of the alienated "people of the land" or
the intransigent upholders of the law. There remains,
amongst others, a serious factor which the reader of the
Gospel has to bear in mind. The Gospels themselves arose out
of a situation of conflict and mission. The early evangelists
found themselves in exactly the same position as Paul—eager
to commend the Gospel in all its grace and freedom, but
constantly inhibited by the attitude of their fellow countrymen, the Jews, who wished to insist on the permanence
and indefectibility of the law of Moses. So could Mark or
Luke have been entirely unaffected by the controversies in
which they were involved as companions of Paul? Are they
honest, painstaking recorders of Jesus' teaching, or does their
account owe something to the desire to make points against
their opponents in the mission field? Are they evangelists in
the cause of the Gospel or propagandists in the cause of the
new Israel? There will be varying answers to these questions.
I content myself with quoting from a passage from *New
Testament Theology* by Jeremias, Volume I, which I happen
to find wholly convincing:

But how reliable is the tradition about Jesus'
attitude to the Torah and the Halakah? The
decisive point to note is that it is unique and
unparalleled in the context of Judaism ... there
can be no question of deriving the radical
statements of Jesus from the primitive community.
For the Palestinian-Syrian church did not continue
Jesus' radical attitude to the ancient law of God.

He goes on to give examples of the way in which the synoptic
Gospels, and Matthew in particular, reflect a rather different
process, i.e. a softening of Jesus' more radical pronoun-
cements in the interests of rapprochement or, as Paul found,
in defence of traditional moral values. I said "and Matthew
in particular" because Jesus' attitude to the law is more fully
and systematically documented in that Gospel than in any of
the others. Anyone who wishes to study this issue in detail
cannot do better than consult Dr. Meier's invaluable treatise
called *Law and History in Matthew's Gospel* (Biblical
Institute Press, Rome).

For myself, therefore, I am satisfied that in the Gospel
narratives we are in the presence of a reliable tradition about
Jesus' attitude to the law which, however enigmatic it
sometimes seems, distinguishes Him as a radical exponent of
the law rather than its destroyer. If in that respect alone, He
is in the tradition of the prophets before Him who, as we
have seen, themselves embrace the law as the very word of
God given at Sinai but distance themselves from the contemporary interpretations of law in order to insist on inward
obedience to it rather than outward observance of it. Their
"thus saith the Lord" was not the enunciation of a new law
but a summons to give meaning and substance to the law
already received. They, like Jesus, could have summarised
the law, though they did not, in the terms—"You are to love
the Lord your God with all your heart and your neighbour as
yourself."

Detailed attention to the text of the Gospels, as they relate
to the law, can never give us plain, unambiguous answers.
We see through a glass of cultural differentiation, language
transference, linguistic obscurities, very darkly indeed. No
two New Testament scholars will come up with precisely the

same answer. The point could hardly be better made than in a judicious statement of Dr. Peter Bläser in Bauer's *Encyclopedia of Biblical Theology.*

> Together with the Old Testament and writers of the later Jewish period, the New Testament evinces the firm conviction that the Old Testament law considered as a whole derives from God as its author. It is, to be sure, called the law of Moses, but Moses is only the mediator of the law (Gal. 3: 20). In the last analysis, it is the law of God (Rom. 7: 22); therefore it is holy and good (Rom. 7: 12, 16). It is an expression of the holy will of God (Rom. 2: 27). Even during the bitter polemic against the judaic element which considered the law as necessary for salvation for those Christian communities converted from paganism, primitive christianity never succumbed to the temptation of solving the problem at issue in the manner of Marcion who denied the divine origin of the Old Testament law. This difficult problem of the law in the New Testament is based directly on the fact that, on the one hand, the divine authority of the law is fully accepted but that on the other hand this same law is no longer in force.
>
> Since the question of the law loomed so large in the early church it was natural that the evangelists, who had the intention at least in some cases of giving answers to questions of actuality in the communities of their day, which answers can be found in the gospels, should give much space to the position of Jesus with regard to the Law of the Old Testament. This position can be studied in the way Jesus acted but, above all, in the dispute-sayings with the scribes and Pharisees and in the basic affirmations of Jesus on the validity of the law. The material which the gospels offer is so varied that it has not been possible so far to reduce all the individual items, which to some extent are intelligible only within the context of a particular situation no longer known to us, to a common

denominator and thus to draw them together into a single presentation. There is, at all events, this dual attitude of Jesus to the mosaic law: acceptance and criticism, faithful observance and transgression are found side by side.

However, we are not entirely dependent on the exact understanding of the words of Jesus; our judgment does not utterly rely on the integrity of the front of us. For the same notes of radical exposition are to be found in His teaching generally and more eloquently still in His actions—neither of which are susceptible to the same extent to subsequent manipulation or conditioning. The parable of the labourer and the vineyard disposes of the claim that awards are given on merit alone (Matthew 20: 1-16). The parable of the sheep and the goats (Matthew 25: 31-46) makes it clear that righteousness is not always what it seems. The parable of the Good Samaritan (Luke 10: 30-35) demonstrates that there is a hierarchy of values; the Priest and the Levite were obeying the law and could justify their seeming callousness for fear of being defiled by a dead body; the Samaritan, an enemy of Judaism, but an observer of the Torah himself, obeyed a higher law in attending to the immediate needs of the man who fell among thieves. He loved his neighbour. The parable of the Prodigal Son (Luke 15: 11-32) shows how a sinner who returns may discover a relationship with God which is hidden from the dutiful observer of His law. The parable of the Pharisee and the publican (Luke 18: 10-14) exposes the difference between the man who pursues righteousness "after the law" and one who throws himself unreservedly on the mercy of God and the gift of forgiveness. But it is never more succinctly put than in this strange little parable buried in the heart of St. Matthew's Gospel:

> "But what do you think about this? A man had two sons. He went to the first, and said, 'My boy, go and work today in the vineyard.' 'I will, sir,' the boy replied; but he never went. The father came to the second and said the same. 'I will not,' he replied, but afterwards he changed his mind and went. Which of these two did as his father

wished?" "The second," they said. Then Jesus answered, "I tell you this: tax-gatherers and prostitutes are entering the kingdom of God ahead of you. For when John came to show you the right way to live, you did not believe him, but the tax-gatherers and prostitutes did; and even when you had seen that, you did not change your minds and believe him." (Matt. 21: 28-32)

I never read this parable without a sense of discomfort—for what matters, Jesus is saying, is not what I appear to do but what I really do. For some of the Pharisees and scribes it was all talk; for some of those whom they despised it was inner obedience to the perceived will of God. Rather surprisingly, it is quite difficult to find a parable which does not, in some way, bear upon Jesus' attitude to the law—and that in itself is significant of the importance of this issue in His life situation as in ours. But His actions are even more eloquent, and it is His actions which primarily provoked opposition from the moral and legal establishment of His day. For easy reference I turn to the conflict stories of St. Mark (1: 1-40 to 3: 1-6). He touched a leper, He forgave sins (without any visible sign of repentance on the part of the sinner), He chose a publican to be one of His disciples, He disregarded the law of fasting, He broke the Sabbath by allowing His disciples to pluck ears of corn and by healing a man in the synagogue on the sabbath day. The passage ends with a highly significant comment by St. Mark:

> On another occasion when he went to synagogue, there was a man in the congregation who had a withered arm; and they were watching to see whether Jesus would cure him on the Sabbath, so that they could bring a charge against him. He said to the man with the withered arm, "Come and stand out here." Then he turned to them: "Is it permitted to do good or to do evil on the Sabbath, to save life or to kill?" They had nothing to say; and, looking round at them with anger and sorrow at their obstinate stupidity, he said to the man, "Stretch out your arm." He stretched it out and his

arm was restored. But the Pharisees, on leaving the synagogue, began plotting against him with the partisans of Herod to see how they could make away with him. (Mark 3: 1-6)

A radical exponent of the law, He did not simply talk about the law, He was eloquent in action, challenging thereby the whole basis of Israel's life as it was commonly understood. Little wonder that at this point Pharisees and Herodians plotted together to destroy Him. Nothing else would have convinced these unlikely allies that they needed to act together.

Perhaps even more striking than His actions were the claims implicit in them, viz. that according to the Synoptic gospels He had power to adjudicate in matters of law, that He spoke for His Father in Heaven when He did so, that He ascended a mountain to proclaim His Torah, that He tells His disciples "to teach what he had commanded" (Matthew 28: 20). St. John goes even further—"you are my friends" He is recorded as saying, "if you do what I command you." At this point I quote some very significant words from Dr. Meier's book, page 165:

Jesus, the fulfiller of Law and prophets, has superseded the Law in the very act of fulfilling it. He can do this because he is not just a Jewish rabbi or a nationalistic Messiah. It is the transcendent Son of God, Son of Man, divine Wisdom, who speaks. With his unique eschatological authority, Jesus dares to replace important provisions of the Torah with his own words.

and from page 169:

The exalted Son of Man closes the gospel by ordering the promulgation and enforcement of all whatsoever he commanded. This whole corpus of Jesus' commands, be they Mosaic or non-Mosaic, is the Christian standard of moral action, the Christian justice which does the Father's will. It contains indeed many elements of the Mosaic Law.

But its validity rests precisely on the authority of
the exalted Son of Man, not on that of Moses. For
the Christian disciple, Jesus is the norm of
morality.

It would seem to me that our conclusions regarding Paul's
attitude to the law will prove to be not dissimilar from the
conclusions I now draw from our study of Jesus' attitude to
the law as we perceive it in the only sources we have, viz. the
Gospels. Like Paul, Jesus is a Jew, believing that salvation is
of the Jews, that they were the Chosen People and that the
law had been given to them on Sinai by the hand of Moses.
Where He is engaged in a Rabbinic-style discussion, He
appeals primarily to the Decalogue though not in the order
with which we are familiar. He summarises the Decalogue in
the famous words, themselves taken from Scripture—"You
are to love the Lord your God with all your heart and mind
and will, and your neighbour as yourself." There is, therefore, a sense in which so far from disparaging the law, He
actually enthrones it and gives it His own authority as the
spokesman of God on earth. But He is confronted not just
with the Decalogue and with the prescriptions that follow
naturally from it: He is confronted with an exceedingly
elaborate, not to say labyrinthine, system of law which has
come to be regarded, if His parables are to be believed, as a
means of salvation and a method of procuring merit in the
sight of God. It was a system which required for its observance massive knowledge, unlimited leisure and inexhaustible
moral resources. Our Lord's mission to His own people, like
Paul's mission to the Gentiles, impressed on His mind the
plight of those hapless Jews, children of Abraham indeed,
who were incapable of knowing, much less observing, the
laws of Israel as they understood them. It had become, as He
said, a burden, a yoke too heavy to be borne by any except the
highly motivated and the exceptionally gifted. He therefore
refers to His own "easy yoke"—easy in the sense that His
Gospel is not so much a demand as a gift, not a call for heroic
self-righteousness in the sight of God as an act of mercy by
God Himself. So He feels free to make distinctions to create a
hierarchy of values (vividly illustrated for example in the
parable of the Good Samaritan). In fact His demands on His

disciples far exceed the demands which contemporary Rabbis would have made upon theirs. Gamaliel or Hillel might well have been satisfied with the young man's claim to have observed the law from his youth. Jesus demands that he should sell all that he has and follow Him. No wonder the young man went sadly away. He ought to have gone to Gamaliel or to Hillel with his question. Our Lord's yoke, therefore, is easier only in the sense that He offers a direct and quite astounding alternative to the traditional route of divine obedience. He cites the commandments for the young man with evident approval but He then offers the royal road to salvation, which is—"follow me". This can only mean that the young man could only be justified, to use Paul's terminology, by faith in Jesus of Nazareth. Our Lord's Gospel of the new relationship with God now available to men, requires on behalf of those who would receive it, faith. It is a mistake to imagine that Paul invented the doctrine of justification by faith. He made use of the familiar terminology but the matter is handled at great depth and under a variety of modes by Jesus Himself. "What shall we do to work the works of God?" the disciples asked. "Believe in Him whom God has sent," He replied—which, in St. John's language, is exactly equivalent to the conversation with the young man, recorded in St. Mark's Gospel. The claims, therefore, which our Lord makes sustain each other and co-inhere. He enthroned the law as delivered (in whatever form) at Sinai, He acknowledges the supreme authority of the God of Israel over all national and individual life, and at the same time He offers His own recension of it (His Torah), and invites men, as a means of walking in the way of God, to faith in Him. The significance of this for mankind as a whole will be discussed in the next chapter, but it would be difficult not to feel that we still have to take the life and example of the words and precepts of Jesus of Nazareth seriously in our attitude to what we are pleased to call "contemporary issues". At the beginning of this chapter we let a man of His own race have the first word. Now we let another man of His own race have the last word:

> Second to none in profundity of insight and grandeur of character, he is in particular an unsur-

passed master of the art of laying bare the inmost
core of spiritual truth and of bringing every issue
back to the essence of religion, the existential
relationship of man and man, and man and God.

Jesus the Jew by Geza Vermes

Utopias now appear to be much more realisable than we had previously thought. We find ourselves nowadays confronted with a question agonising in quite a different way: How can we avoid their final realisation?

Nicholas Berdyaev

A lot of the English ... have left behind the challenging rocks of discipline by circumstance, yet cannot reach the shining plateau of self-discipline, and their freedom only entangles them with whims and fancies, silliness and self-indulgence.

J. B. Priestley
Prescription for Our Time

XI

Promised Land

In which direction, in this twentieth-century wilderness, lies the Promised Land? Capitalism, however successful as a means of production, however indispensable, some would say in raising living standards, is hardly sufficient as a philosophy of life. There is little in it to put a song in your heart, or quicken your step. Mr. Lowry's paintings of the industrial scene in the north of England may be difficult to identify precisely on the ground, but it represents a wilderness experience in his own mind—the towering chimneys, the hilly streets, the polluted rivers, the ramshackle terrace houses and the tiny matchstick men who inhabit the land. Law reigns indeed but the iron law of profit not the law, so it would seem, of a Heavenly Father intent upon the growth and happiness of His children. But then what reality remains either in the Promised Land of liberal democracy? Of the 127 nation states in the world, ninety-seven are, we are told, either blatantly totalitarian of the right or the left, or single party systems. That tide has ebbed, leaving only a few tide marks to show the golden limits to which our forefathers aspired. And even within those systems which rightly call themselves free, there has been a serious loss of nerve, and a certain kind of freedom is purchased at too high a price, leaving the honest citizen desperately vulnerable to the violent, the powerful, the unscrupulous, the adventurers. Lord Hailsham, in his book *Dilemma of Democracy* puts it thus:

> For some years now, and especially since February 1974, I have been oppressed by a sinister foreboding. We are living in the City of Destruction, a dying country in a dying civilization, and across the plain there is no wicket gate offering a way of escape. We have to stay here and fight it out.

Indeed we must do so for the sake of our children. I
do not say the situation is hopeless. Indeed, if I
thought so I would not trouble to write. But, if we
go on as we are, I can see nothing but disaster
ahead, though I am quite unable to predict either
when, or exactly how, it will overtake us ... This
does not mean that I have abandoned faith in our
traditions or institutions. I continue to believe in
democracy and wish for more of it rather than less.
But the evidence to the contrary is profoundly
discouraging. Democracy has a very bad track
record. Among forms of human government, it has
been the rare exception and, where it has emerged,
it has always seemed to carry within it the seeds of
its own destruction. It has been short-lived. Even
where it has not succumbed to external aggression,
it has proved unable to withstand or defend itself
against pressures from within, the spendthrifts who
disperse its resources, the class warriors who break
up its unity, the separatists who try to divide it
geographically, the lobbies and pressure groups
who try to cajole, corrupt or intimidate its governments, the political parties who undo or undermine
each other's activities.

The chapter is headed "The City of Destruction". It does not
seem that the Promised Land lies in this direction. But what
of that philosophy of life which has captured the more ardent
spirits of the twentieth century and challenged, as no other
philosophy has, the intellectual and economic status quo in
which many of us were brought up? Half the world lives
under the banner of the Hammer and the Sickle, and our
literature is loaded with the memories of those who nobly
embraced that cause in the belief that there lay the Promised
Land. They embraced it nobly and often adhered to it
through years of deepening disillusionment. In 1977 a man
aged eighty-four found it necessary to write to President
Brezhnev resigning his membership of the Communist Party
after fifty years of devoted service to it. And the reason? He
could no longer endure the contradictions in his own mind
between what he had hoped for and what he now perceived.

Fifty years in the wilderness, fighting battles, accepting hardships, spurning domestic delights—and the Promised Land proved to be a grey Utopia, oppressive, inefficient, politically pragmatic, as cruel as the Tsarism they thought they had left behind. That was the judgment of a simple Party member. I quote now from the third volume of Dr. Kolakowski's recent work on Marxism. The volume is entitled *The Breakdown* :

> Marxism has been frozen and immobilized for decades as the ideological superstructure of a totalitarian political movement, and in consequence has lost touch with intellectual developments and social realities. The hope that it could be revived and made fruitful once again soon proved to be an illusion. As an explanatory "system" it is dead, nor does it offer any "method" that can be effectively used to interpret modern life, to foresee the future, or cultivate utopian projections. Contemporary Marxist literature, although plentiful in quantity, has a depressing air of sterility and helplessness, in so far as it is not purely historical.
>
> The effectiveness of Marxism as an instrument of political mobilization is quite another matter. As we have seen, its terminology is used in support of the most variegated political interests. In the Communist countries of Europe, where Marxism is the official legitimation of the existing regimes, it has virtually lost all conviction, while in China it has been deformed out of recognition. Wherever Communism is in power, the ruling class transforms it into an ideology whose real sources are nationalism, racism, or imperialism. Communism has done much to strengthen nationalist ideologies by using them to seize power or hold on to it, and in this way it has produced its own gravediggers. Nationalism lives only as an ideology of hate, envy, and thirst for power; as such it is a disruptive element in the Communist world, the coherence of which is based on force. If the whole world were Communist it would either have to be dominated by a single

imperialism, or there would be an unending series of wars between the "Marxist" rulers of different countries.

We are witnesses and participators in momentous and complicated intellectual and moral processes, the combined effects of which cannot be foreseen. On the one hand, many optimistic assumptions of nineteenth-century humanism have broken down, and in many fields of culture there is a sense of bankruptcy. On the other hand, thanks to the unprecedented speed and diffusion of information, human aspirations throughout the world are increasing faster than the means of satisfying them; this leads to rapidly growing frustration and consequent aggressiveness. Communists have shown great skill in exploiting this state of mind and channelling aggressive feelings in various directions according to circumstances, using fragments of Marxist language to suit their purpose. Messianic hopes are the counterpart of the sense of despair and impotence that overcomes mankind at the sight of its own failures. The optimistic belief that there is a ready-made, immediate answer to all problems and misfortunes, and that only the malevolence of enemies (defined according to choice) stands in the way of its being instantly applied, is a frequent ingredient in ideological systems passing under the name of Marxism—which is to say that Marxism changes content from one situation to another and is cross-bred with other ideological traditions. At present Marxism neither interprets the world nor changes it: it is merely a repertoire of slogans' serving to organize various interests, most of them completely remote from those with which Marxism originally identified itself. A century after the collapse of the First International, the prospect of a new International capable of defending the interests of oppressed humanity throughout the world is less likely than it has ever been.

The self-deification of mankind, to which Marxism gave philosophical expression, has ended

in the same way as all such attempts, whether
individual or collective: it has revealed itself as the
farcical aspect of human bondage.

I make no apologies for that long quotation, it rings down the
curtain on a splendid but wholly misleading enterprise in
pursuit of a Promised Land. But is there indeed any such
thing? Do we not deceive ourselves in this wilderness with
dreams of milk and honey, peaceful days and golden
evenings? Is this not just the familiar language of the Utopias
of a hundred imaginations, part of the escapist literature of
mankind? This is what Paul Turner has to say in his edition
of Thomas More's *Utopia* :

> Utopias have been written to illustrate many
> different theories of perfection. In *Christianopolis*
> the secret of happiness is true religion; in William
> Morris's *News from Nowhere* (1890) it is social-
> ism. In Samuel Gott's *New Jerusalem* (1648) it is
> education: teachers at the university get "maximum
> salaries", and the students take down lecture-notes
> in shorthand. In Tommaso Campanella's *City of
> the Sun* (1623) the good life is largely a matter of
> eugenics:
>   To this vein of pure wishful thinking Plato adds
> the element of serious political theory. In the
> *Republic* Socrates works out the idea of a perfect
> state, which embodies the principle of justice, and
> includes the communal ownership of goods and of
> women. The next stage in the development of the
> form is to give this airy nothing a local habitation
> and a name. In the *Timaeus* it is located on the
> island of Atlantis, which sank beneath the sea about
> nine thousand years before; and in the *Critias* the
> island is described in detail. It consists of several
> concentric rings of land, separated by circular
> canals which are so inter-connected that ships can
> sail right into the interior, and anchor there in
> underground harbours. Among other practical con-
> veniences are two springs, one h. and one c., from
> which water is distributed all over the island

through pipes attached, where necessary, to the bridges that cross the canals; and the outermost ring of land is very useful as a race-course.

Perhaps, after all, the Promised Land is just a Hebrew variant of the paradise myth, expressed in a different way in *The Epic of Gilgamesh,* the product of the same cultural environment as the Hebrews.

The croak of the raven was not heard, the bird of death did not utter the cry of death, the lion did not devour, the wolf did not tear the lamb, the dove did not mourn, there was no widow, no sickness, no old age, no lamentation.

That question the reader can only answer for himself. But his answer must take account of the strangely sober realistic view of the Promised Land which emerges from the literature we have been studying. It existed; it was called Canaan; it was the size of Wales; it was, in those days before exploitive agriculture destroyed it, a land rich in vegetation with plentiful water and mighty forests. When the spies returned to the people in the wilderness they brought with them bunches of grapes, pomegranates and figs. It was a good land indeed, which flowed with milk and honey. But to the Hebrew people the Promised Land was more than a geographical location, lying somewhere between latitudes 30 and 35. It was to be a human experience, lying on the other side of Sinai; it could be anywhere, but they could never have subscribed to the view that it was nowhere, a mere Utopia, the figment of a frustrated mind. It had a political shape, social contours, a moral climate, intellectual heights. The one thing certain about it was that it lay on the other side of Sinai. May I, for the sake of clarity, summarise the process which we have discovered in Hebrew history and Hebrew thought, as it is expressed in their sacred Scriptures? The escape from Egypt (the actuality of which I find impossible to doubt) was an act of liberation, so they believed, initiated by their God whose name, Jahwe, was vouchsafed to them. It constituted liberation from the arbitrary legal system which obtained in Egypt and sanctioned slavery, and prepared the way for freedom—freedom "in the wilderness". Any man can be free in the wilderness if he is able to survive there. But freedom, so it would seem, is only safe for mankind in so far as it is exercised within an authoritative framework of accepted behaviour. No society will survive in the wilderness without guidelines, signposts, visible paths, prescribed objectives. So Moses received on their behalf, by means wholly mysterious to us, although coolly narrated by them, a series of words, divine words he believed, for the instruction of the infant community. These "words" have been preserved for posterity, slightly amended and not wholly clear, as the indefectible basis of law-making, Hebrew, Roman, Christian, Western. But the mighty development of the legal system must not obscure for us the nature of the original Commandments. They were positive (though expressed in a negative way), definite, authoritative and eternal.

In the grounds of Brandon Castle in southern Ireland there grows a chestnut tree said to be the biggest in the British Isles. As far as I am concerned it could be the biggest in the world. At a rough estimate a hundred sheep could shelter under it. The lateral growth of the lower branches has been so stupendous that the branches themselves have sunk into the ground at various points, giving the impression of being themselves separate trees. I saw it on a beautiful late summer day with the sun shining brightly on the ruined battlements of the castle. Under the tree it was dark; nothing grew there; it was a jungle in itself. But there was a central stem, in itself not very large, quite difficult to find and identify as the central stem. Centuries before, it had been a sapling standing in open ground, staked for protection against the wind with the grass green and springing around it. Now it filled the earth. That for me was a picture of the development—gross development some people might call it—of a huge body of law which fills the earth but had its origin in an obscure, wholly mysterious event in the wilderness of Sinai. It would be vain now to lop the branches but important nevertheless to perceive the trunk. There is a certain simplicity about those ten words which rebukes our casuistry, our easy moralising, our unwitting compromises.

It is certain that chronologically the Promised Land stood the other side of Sinai. It suggests that the Promised Land may indeed flow with milk and honey but if it is to be healthful for those who live in it it must embody a certain view of life which accords to an authority higher than ours a certain reverence. Freedom is to be enjoyed within certain moral and spiritual boundaries prescribed for us—with our happiness and social harmony as its objective. The prophets, former and latter, bear witness to the fact that the people of Israel lived very uneasily, and for a greater part without much conviction, within these boundaries. Every prophet, without exception, found it necessary to draw the attention of rulers and subjects alike to the flagrant disregard for the basic law of God. The land (the Promised Land at that stage) was full of robbery, lies and violence.

> Why has the land become a dead land, scorched like the desert and untrodden? The Lord said, It is because they forsook my law which I set before them; they neither obeyed me nor conformed to it. They followed the promptings of their own stubborn hearts, they followed the Baalim as their forefathers had taught them. Therefore these are the words of the Lord of Hosts the God of Israel: I will feed this people with wormwood and give them bitter poison to drink. I will scatter them among nations whom neither they nor their forefathers have known; I will harry them with the sword until I have made an end of them. (Jer. 9: 12-16)

The fate which Jeremiah had foreseen as a consequence of their neglect of the law of God in the Promised Land came to pass within a few years of the prophecy. The Promised Land, now only a tiny enclave of the Canaan which had been promised to Abraham, was occupied by enemy forces and the Jewish State effectively perished. Thereafter the Promised Land had perforce to take a different shape, had to summon up a different set of images. The dream of observing God's merciful law in their own land as an object lesson to the nations of the world died the death. The rest of Hebrew history is a record of how the Hebrews attempted to come to terms with this reality. They perceived their Promised Land in the ghettoes of the cities of the ancient world, seeking so to

extend, and sometimes to qualify the ancient law of Sinai as
to be able to observe it in a heathen environment. They
pursued it as far as the shores of the Dead Sea—an
inhospitable land indeed without milk or honey, but safe, so
they believed, from the insidious influences of Hellenism—
there to pursue salvation by minute obedience to the law
which, for all its growth and elaboration, they still attributed
to the hand of Moses at Sinai. They pursued it in the
Palestine of the British mandate until once more they
possessed the ancient land and revived the ancient nation—
but without calling for obedience to the ancient law. Israel is,
by definition, a secular state. Dr. Immanuel Jakobovits in his
book *The Timely and the Timeless* has this to say about the
latest version of the Promised Land:

> Paradoxically, while the establishment of the
> Jewish State has greatly intensified Jewish con-
> sciousness and identification in communities every-
> where, it has also weakened the main common
> denominator between them. In the Diaspora, many
> Jews have found vicarious refuge for the expression
> of their Jewish identity in the existence and support
> of Israel. For them, living as Jews by proxy has
> conveniently replaced the personal discipline of
> Jewish living. In Israel, again, large numbers of
> Jews have found in their national allegiance a
> substitute for traditional Jewish loyalties. For these
> Jews, the Diaspora became the vicarious haven of
> their residual Jewishness, as poignantly attested by
> the many Israelis who discover their Jewish feeling
> and identity only when they visit the Diaspora and
> find communication with their faith and with
> fellow-Jews in the synagogue. Thus Jewish
> statehood helped to accelerate the secularisation, or
> de-spiritualisation, of Jewish life both at home and
> abroad, leading to an ever widening gap between
> Jews and Judaism.
>
> The Yom Kippur War will force us to recognise
> that a secularist Jewish State, itself a contradiction
> in terms, cannot be viable in the long run, as we
> will find the ultimate answer to many of our most

pressing problems in a growing emphasis on our spiritual assets.

Does the Hebrew hope of a Promised Land, therefore, prove as illusory as every other hope? Is it just another Utopia in a depressing series of Utopias? If that is so, then Jews and Christians, and Marxists and Humanists as well, have to face some disconcerting questions. Jews will have to admit the possibility that their understanding of the course of their history has proved entirely erroneous. They were not God's Chosen People after all but just another Semitic clan who happened to survive through a combination of circumstance and hereditary skills. It will follow, for Christians, that Jesus of Nazareth and Saul of Tarsus were also mistaken. There was no old Israel. There is no new Israel. The controversy about the law would be proved to be meaningless. We are entirely without a law binding on the conscience of mankind—and therefore without a Gospel; for the Gospel, as both Jesus and Paul understood it, was the Good News of new resources available through faith in Christ to those who wished to walk in God's way and live by His revealed will. Humanists and Marxists will have to speak for themselves. But Marx was a Jew and many of his characteristic beliefs arise, however paradoxically, from his Jewish background. Humanists will have relied, perhaps more than they thought, for their liberal hopes on the expansive, hopeful, forward-looking stance which is typical of the Hebraeo-Christian tradition at its best. Brothers and comrades, we are all in the wilderness and it looks as if we are going to be there for ever. The Promised Land recedes as we approach it; the oasis to which we have struggled for water and food proves to be a mirage. Everywhere is sand, and heat, and blinding storms, and the carrion birds circle above us waiting for our collapse. Is there anything to be saved from this wreckage of our ancient long-disappointed hopes?

It would be possible to say that the Scriptures themselves bear witness to the wrong turning which the people of Israel took. By the time of our Lord the so-called law had become a burden too heavy to be borne by natural men. It had become an obstacle race which only moral and spiritual athletes could hope to complete. It was not concerned so much with a harmonious society and creative relationships as with a prescribed method of achieving and maintaining moral and spiritual superiority. It was a means of acquiring merit in God's sight; a method by which you maintained the view that you were not as other men. Now however persuasive the arguments on the other side may be—and I have acknowledged them earlier in this book—I have to regard that development as the blindest of blind alleys. It leads ineluctably to Qumran and to death. In that form and with that intention the law had nothing to say to anyone other than the fanatic and the devotee. It was the law of a sect, not a law for all mankind. Jesus of Nazareth and Saul of Tarsus, themselves practising Jews, were surely right—a Jewish community, devoted to that objective, could only bring down the wrath of God and the wrath of man upon it. Jesus saw Jerusalem ringed with armies—not the Hosts of Heaven, but the vengeful hosts of earth.

I hope it will have emerged from reading the chapters relating to the early stages of the law, as they were reflected in the writings of the former and latter prophets, that the law may be understood not just in terms of demand but in terms of succour. The words entrusted to Moses at Sinai were a loving provision of God for the needs of His people, needs of which they were largely unaware but which became more and more clamant as they tangled with the alien rituals and the political forces of the near middle-east world. God, so Hosea says, took His child by the hand in the wilderness and taught him how to walk—before he was required to run. "You shall hear ... a voice behind you," Isaiah said "saying, This is the way, follow it" (Isaiah 30: 21). Even if we are entirely sceptical about the way in which it is supposed that the ten words were made known to man, we could hardly deny that they constitute a moral and social programme which could materially advance the cause of human kind and remove some at least of our most dangerous social distempers. You are not to murder, not to steal, not to commit adultery, not to bear false witness, not to covet. Put them in any order you like—if they were taken seriously men might enjoy freedoms which at the moment are denied them by the depredations of their fellow man and the seemingly uncontrollable drives of their own nature.

Stephen Mayor has written a book called *Paradise Defined* which he might as well have called the "Promised Land". In it he distinguishes certain elements which he believes to be essential not simply to Christian society but to society as a whole. He enumerates these elements as follows:

1.   What a Christian society is not
2.   A society founded on Christian principles
3.   An open society
4.   A society which recognises sin
5.   A society which can deal with collective sin
6.   A society which recognises the ambiguity of progress
7.   A society which knows the proper place of Law

Under this last heading he makes the following comment:

> If a society which gives supreme place to law is less than Christian, so is a society which is without law. Strictly speaking, there can be no society without law. Any society, political or of any other kind, is held together only because it has rules of behaviour and some sort of sanctions (even if only black looks) to be employed against those who break them. But there are some people who think that law is a bad thing, and that ideally society should be without it, even if the ideal is pretty impracticable.
>
> This is a Utopian ideal. Perhaps something like it appears in the Marxist anticipation that in communism the State will "wither away". Marxists have in general been a good deal less precise about conditions in the future communist world than about the evils they condemn in the present capitalist world, but that the State should "wither away" looks pretty Utopian. The so-called socialist part of the world, where the revolution is past and communism is nearer, seems to be making slow progress towards this improbable ideal. But many Christians have cherished similar ideals. They look forward to a time when the State, and law, the

expression of the authority of the State, exist no more. Sectarian Christian groups have attempted from time to time to set up societies without law, and many more Christians have had rather guilty feelings about the fact that law is still needed in so-called Christian countries.

But there is no justification for such feelings of guilt. If a society without law is an impossibility it cannot be a desirable ideal. There are enough possible things to work for without setting ourselves to attain the unattainable. The hope of doing without law arises out of experience of the harshness of law hitherto, or even of the corruption and injustice of law. The Marxist hope of seeing the State wither away arises out of the belief that all the states so far have been instruments of class-oppression and all laws designed to protect class interests. With due allowance for exaggeration that may be true. The remedy is to work gradually towards more just and more merciful laws, not the hopeless quest for life without law.

"The remedy is to work gradually towards more just and more merciful laws," Stephen Mayor says. Perhaps it is in this direction that the Promised Land lies. So at least it would seem to be in the teaching of Jesus. His teaching is remarkable not in the sense that He disparaged the law (although His opponents found it easy to make out that He did so), but in that He gave it an unexampled depth and range. To quote Stephen Mayor again, "He discerned behind all the detailed regulations a single purpose: the creation of a holy and loving community." The monstrous lateral development of the law which characterised later Judaism is replaced in His teaching by a powerful vertical development. On the one hand it is vertical downwards in the sense that He insists on the inner and ultimate significance of the Decalogue for human life and society. Thus He says:

You have learned that our forefathers were told, "Do not commit murder; anyone who commits murder must be brought to judgment." But what I tell you is this: Anyone who nurses anger against his brother must be brought to judgment. If he abuses his brother he must answer for it to the court; if he sneers at him he will have to answer for it in the fires of hell.

If when you are bringing your gift to the altar, you suddenly remember that your brother has a grievance against you, leave your gift where it is before the altar. First go and make your peace with your brother, and only then come back and offer your gift.

If someone sues you, come to terms with him promptly while you are both on your way to court; otherwise he may hand you over to the judge, and the judge to the constable, and you will be put in jail. I tell you, once you are there you will not be let out till you have paid the last farthing.

You have learned that they were told, "Do not commit adultery." But what I tell you is this: If a man looks on a woman with a lustful eye, he has already committed adultery with her in his heart.

If your right eye is your undoing, tear it out and fling it away; it is better for you to lose one part of your body than for the whole of it to be thrown into hell. And if your right hand is your undoing, cut it off and fling it away; it is better for you to lose one part of your body than for the whole of it to go to hell.

They were told, "A man who divorces his wife must give her a note of dismissal." But what I tell you is this: If a man divorces his wife for any cause other than unchastity he involves her in adultery; and anyone who marries a divorced woman commits adultery.

Again, you have learned that our forefathers were told, "Do not break your oath", and, "Oaths sworn to the Lord must be kept." But what I tell you is this: You are not to swear at all—not by heaven, for it is God's throne, nor by earth, for it is his footstool, nor by Jerusalem, for it is the city of the great King, nor by your own head, because you cannot turn one hair of it white or black. Plain "Yes" or "No" is all you need to say; anything beyond that comes from the devil.

You have learned that they were told, "Eye for eye, tooth for tooth." But what I tell you is this: Do not set yourself against the man who wrongs you. If someone slaps you on the right cheek, turn and offer him your left. If a man wants to sue you for your shirt, let him have your coat as well. If a man in authority makes you go one mile, go with him two. Give when you are asked to give; and do not turn your back on a man who wants to borrow.

You have learned that they were told, "Love your neighbour, hate your enemy." But what I tell you is this: Love your enemies and pray for your persecutors; only so can you be children of your heavenly Father, who makes his sun rise on good and bad alike, and sends the rain on the honest and the dishonest. If you love only those who love you, what reward can you expect? Surely the tax-gatherers do as much as that. And if you greet only your brothers, what is there extraordinary about that? Even the heathen do as much. There must be no limit to your goodness, as your heavenly Father's goodness knows no bounds." (Matt. 5: 21-48)

On the other hand, He gives to the law a strong upward thrust. Perhaps that phrase needs a certain explanation. It has to be said that in some expressions of Judaism the law had replaced the God who gave it; it had become an object of devotion; to obey the law was to obey God; to love it was to love God; to ignore it was to ignore God. Jesus revived what is surely the older concept—that the law is an expression of God's loving mercy and concern. We receive the law and look up into the eyes of God. We carry the law with our right hand but the left hand is in the hand of God; we study the law but our eyes are on the Promised Land. For Christ, the law was intended as a mediator between God and man, a channel of communication, a transcript of the Divine voice at Sinai. That He presumed to go further than that and to enthrone the law in His own person as Messiah does not dispose of the fact that He first acknowledged the "ten words" in all their range and depth as a God-given prescription for the life of all mankind on the face of the earth. God's will for all mankind, expressed in the ten words at Sinai, is now expressed in the Word of God Himself. He came not to destroy but to fulfil.

Pilgrims through this barren land, this wilderness partly of our own making, partly the result of natural features over which we have no control, need to feel that their journey is necessary. Life without the Promised Land is a burden too heavy to be borne by most of us. We are not built that way. So I end this chapter with two quotations from Joy Davidman's book *Smoke on the Mountain*—all the more significant perhaps because she was a Jewess and a member of the Communist party before she became a practising Christian. The first quotation comes early on in the book:

> When Sinai flamed and thundered, the Children of Israel were indeed briefly afraid. Apparently nothing short of a volcano, however, could intimidate them long enough to make them re-examine the code by which they lived. They were lusty and lustful men; they heartily enjoyed their hewings and smitings and woman stealings; and if they got killed on their forays—well, if you sat in the tent and worried about that you were as good as dead already. A safe life was unthinkable to them— nobody had ever told them that they were entitled to social security. Even the love of God which was entering their hearts was no gentle thing, but the fierce love of a strong man for a stronger master.
>
> The discovery that he was a God of justice must have given them a profound spiritual shock; it seemed, then, that there were things a man shouldn't enjoy!
>
> Shock; and also exultation, for the Decalogue raised them above the trivial level of enjoyment, gave life a shape, a purpose, a plan. Though previous Eastern cultures had struggled upward temporarily to some knowledge that justice pleased

the gods, it is on the thunderstone of the Tablets
that Western civilisation has built its house. If the
house is tottering today, we can scarcely steady it by
pulling the foundation out from under.

The second quotation is from the end of the book:

And perhaps Christianity, if we ever embrace it not
for our own worldly advantage but through surrender to God, will not only enable us to obey the Ten
Commandments but enable us to enjoy it; not only
save this transitory world for the few perplexed
years we spend in it, but bring us out of this noise
and darkness and helplessness and terror that we
call the world into the full Light: Light we remember from our childhood dreams, and from glimpses
through music and art and the ecstasy of first love;
Light we have known through a brief glow in our
few moments of really selfless charity; Light which,
in our secret hearts, we desire more than money
and sex and power and the pride of the self. We
men are all thieves who have stolen the self which
was meant as a part of God and tried to keep it for
ourselves alone. But if we give it up again, we
might hear the words he spoke to a penitent thief
once: "Today shalt thou be with me in paradise."

Ah, mon cher, for anyone who is alone, without God and without a master, the weight of days is dreadful. Hence one must choose a master, God being out of style.

Albert Camus
The Fall

XII

Ten Considerations

To those of you who have struggled through the jungle thus far, I offer a little clearing in the jungle from which we may contemplate the path we have taken and try to discern the path that lies ahead. We have found our way, not inerrantly indeed, but I trust without serious deviations, through the history and literature of an ancient people, the Jews. When the biblical scholars have had their say about the documents and historians have had their say about the history, it remains true that the law played a dominant part in making Israel what it was. Whatever the origin of that law, it has remained the datum point in Jewish history for over three thousand years. It may have been honoured more in the breach than in the observance but it stands there still challenging our easy assumptions and pious hopes with the stern unchanging word of God. That word was indeed often obscured, and sometimes submerged, by the easy casuistry of men but there were always those in the history of Israel, inspired by God so they believed, to recall the people to their first love, their primal obedience. Prophets stood against kings reminding them of the words from Sinai. A Josiah here and an Ezra there, were raised up to enthrone again the ancient law in the life of the people. Fervent spirits, threatened by the paganism of the Diaspora, created little communities in which they studied and observed the law with heroic dedication. Even under the dynamic influence of a new religion, the law held its own as the archetypal word of God, taking its place in the early catechisms of the Church, recited in its liturgy, displayed in its buildings. Paul, in all the tempestuous enthusiasm of a new-found faith, and involved in bitter controversy with the orthodox practitioners of the law, nevertheless could never shake himself free of it. The law, he said, is holy and good. Jesus Himself, with a wide-ranging view of Israel's history and an instinctive understanding of the Sacred Scriptures, devastatingly critical as He was of the representatives of the law in His day, nevertheless continued to see in the law the very word of God designed for our blessing and our peace. Under His loving hand the old, heavy, grinding yoke of ancient Israel was to become the easy yoke of a new Israel. But it remained a yoke, which every believer had to wear. Even if we dissent altogether from Israel's view of itself, as reflected in the Sacred Scriptures, we cannot deny that Israel exists, and that it offers to the world a highly distinctive view of the place of law in society. As historians, or sociologists, or jurists, we cannot afford to neglect a source so rich, so comprehensive, so diverse, so persistent. The wells may have been silted up but we can still find water there. In a world full of problems, and short of solutions, any illumination is better than none.

But these same historians, sociologists or jurists have a right to ask the question, So what? You have proved it up to the hilt and it doesn't mean a thing. From this clearing then we would wish to discern at least a general sense of direction. To do so seriously would require another book, or shall we say, a second volume; for no one who writes about the place of law in society can begin to do so without traversing the ground I have traversed. He may find for himself a quite different path through this jungle but he will have to find a path. He will need the benefit of the past if he is himself to benefit the future. I am not a historian, a sociologist or a jurist. The second volume, therefore, will have to be written by someone else but I bequeath to him certain elementary considerations which have arisen in my mind as I have pursued this study. They relate to society as a whole (of which I am a citizen), to the Church (of which I am a member), to the individual, humanist and Christian (all of which I aspire to be). What then is the bearing of the experience of Israel in the wilderness upon our own lives, social and personal, in our particular wilderness?

Society

1

Israel represented at the same time a religious and political entity; it was a Church and a nation. David was not just a king, he was High Priest. The law which he was responsible for administering was, in his view, divinely sanctioned as the way of life for his nation. Church and state were inseparable. He marched before his armies and he danced before the ark containing the two tablets of stone. Politically, this equation is no longer possible, and never has been possible since "Christendom" collapsed into a series of competing nation states, erecting their own legal systems, choosing their own religion. But this ought not to obscure from us the fact that Israel represented a positive and coherent conviction that every nation, not just their nation, was under the law of God—their God, who was, at the same time, the God of all mankind, largely unrecognised, seldom accepted as such. They held a law of a God of all the earth in trust not just for the Church but for the nation. The issues I have been discussing therefore, in their view confront not just a Chosen People but society as a whole everywhere, and at all times. It is a strange and indisputable fact that the law conceived within the heart of a tiny middle-eastern people should, via various agencies, have influenced the legal systems and the life-styles of most of the great nations of the world.

2

The Commandments were the expression of a will and purpose for the body corporate and not primarily for individuals. They constituted the matter of a covenant or, as it is sometimes called, a treaty, between a subject people and their Suzerain. Disobedience to the law did not simply result in damage to an individual member of that subject body; it threatened the life of the nation. There was no such thing as a private morality. Murder, adultery, dishonouring of parents, false witness, threatened the treaty and provoked the wrath of the Suzerain. Punishment, whatever form it took, was not so much an act of vengeance, or even of correction, as a public disowning of a breach of the divine law. Disobedience to the Suzerain threatened the whole edifice of society. The notion of "consenting adults" would have seemed meaningless. What mattered was not whether adults consented to a particular course of action but whether the course of action was in line with the revealed will. Governments were not free to alter or to ignore the covenant statutes to make them more convenient, or to mollify public opinion. They were guardians of an unchanging law which they might indeed re-apply but could never ignore. The king who found the law book in the temple reacted with consternation to the thought that he had, even unwittingly, ignored the law of God and unwittingly brought down the law of God upon his nation. To the Jews law-making, therefore, could never be just a matter of convenience, or an expedient; it did not bend to public opinion but formed it. It had to take account of local conditions indeed but it could not, in so doing, minimise or eviscerate the law originally given. To do so, the Hebrews would have said, is to imperil society as such, to make it ungovernable, to expose it to chaos.

3

Every system of law requires casuistry to make it workable, that is to say, the universal words committed to Israel by the hand of Moses have to be made particular to a nation, to a culture, to an epoch. The elaboration of the law in the life of Israel was not just a mistake, although it produced exceedingly unfortunate results; it was an attempt to make the general particular, to help the Jew to know what he was to do about the Commandments when he sought to obey them, not in the wilderness or in Canaan, but in Alexandria or France or Britain. The unmistakable laws of God are given on the mountain but they have to be brought down to the plain—and in the process run the danger of losing their sharpness and their universality. That is why the prophets, Saul of Tarsus and Jesus of Nazareth, were consistent with each other in always appealing back to the universal as a corrective to the casuistry which had developed in applying it to the particular. But every generation has to rethink the implications of the universal law, nevertheless, if that law is to be a practical guide to governments and individuals. The "situation ethic" exposes itself to criticism and becomes illegitimate only when it loses its hold on certain identifiable moral principles. To be an "ethic" at all it must take account of the situation, make sense in our particular wilderness. This requires that there should be voices in every society raised to remind us of the absolute in a sea of relativities. It is never right to commit adultery or, as our Lord said, to lust after a woman in your heart. It is never right to murder or, as our Lord said, to be angry with your brother. It is never right to forswear yourself or, as our Lord said, to take refuge in ambiguity. These are not just offences against people, fellow members of the race, they are offences against the law of God and put society at risk. For many a government there awaits the discovery of the law of God in some temple or other, challenging their current practice, exposing their pretensions and questioning the validity of their policies. The discovery of that ancient law was unhappily too late to save Israel from the consequences of their blatant lawlessness and the foolish public policies that flowed from it. From many a temple the guardians of the law look out upon a world seemingly hell-bent on destruction, but they are not heard. Like Jeremiah, they lament the blindness of their leaders and wait for the end.

4

It would be wholly unrealistic to suppose that in the process of particularisation a code of law could ever be produced equally acceptable across a nation or a commonwealth of nations. Diversity, disagreement, opposition are inevitable. But even the attempt to apply the universal to the particular is of great consequence in the psychological aspects of corporate life. For to apply to the particular is to assent to the universal. We do not have to believe in the God of Israel, or the God of Christians, or the God of Islam, before we may recognise certain universals which seem to be indispensable to human society. If we cannot appeal to the authority of God for our universals, we can at least appeal to the consistent testimony of human history, the experience of the race. Given that background assumption, we shall not be inventing laws, we shall be searching for them; we shall not be opening up new wells, we shall be uncovering the old; we shall not be appealing for new insights, we shall be recovering old ones. In short, we shall not allow ourselves to be trapped in our national or cultural habitat and presume that our circumstances are wholly peculiar to ourselves; we shall be exposing our judgments of what is, or is not, legitimate to the judgment of the human race or, if we may go so far, to the God and Creator of the human race. A lot of our disorders, social and moral, would then be seen for what they are— dis-orders, the consequences of a mistaken understanding of universal principles. Give the Hebrews their due; they were as imperfect, as nefarious, as any other race on earth, but they could never close their ears entirely to the thunders from Sinai. They lived under the shadow of the law even when they did not observe it; they were conscious of a God of justice even when they meted out injustice to their fellow men. So, they would say, the dignity of the law and its authority over the conscience can never depend just on solemn procedures of a court, or the wisdom and integrity of a judge, or the power of Parliament; when you take the oath you are calling Heaven to witness the authority and antiquity of the law; when you stand in the dock you stand in the presence of the God of law—and of mercy; when you commit a man to prison you are invoking once more the sanctions that came down from Sinai. Even to be aware of that, however little you may regard it in practice, is to enter into the mind and share the experience of the Children of Israel who have lived by that truth for three thousand years. There are not many Jews in prison, not many Jewish boys in the court, not many Jewish girls in need of care and protection, not many Jewish patriarchs eking out a miserable existence in some unhappy home for elderly people. The Jews are no better than anyone else; they face the same temptations; they suffer the same disasters, but they live still under the shadow of Sinai and they hear the voice of God in the law of the land.

The Church

5

When the Church and society are no longer co-extensive, when the Sovereign of the realm is no longer the high priest, then the Church has to gather to itself a particular role—even if it has no wish to accept extra responsibilities. It becomes, amongst other things, the guardian of the law—in exactly the sense in which the prophets of Israel, under the pressures of social disintegration, had to take to themselves the responsibility which more properly belonged to the whole community. They, and their successors, the scribes, became exponents of the law. The Pharisees, for all their unhappy reputation, were genuinely guardians of the law of God, seeking constantly to apply it to government policy, social action and everyday life. Of course the Church is always in danger of becoming the Pharisee, calling for wholly unrealistic policies, condemning wholly imaginary wrongs and making obedience to the will of a loving God an odiously heavy burden to be borne, at best with resignation, at worst with bitter resentment. But the fact that the Church may misrepresent its role does not mean that it can dispose of it. We are long past the stage when we can unthinkingly reiterate the ancient law and expect people to respond to it. But we can, after the manner of our Lord Himself, rescue the law from its association with dour uncomprehending obedience and make it once more a joy and a resource, a welcome voice in the ear, a reassuring signpost in the wilderness. This may properly be called the prophetic rule of the Church, i.e. to do what the prophets did, to attempt to naturalise the beneficent law of a loving God in the life of the people, to turn in this way and that like a diamond, to catch a glint of the light that flowed from Sinai. We are puzzled people, we of the West, so competent with technological hardware, so amateur in our judgments about the end and purpose of existence and how it is to be pursued. As I look from where I am sitting in the study I can see a dozen books on my own shelves instructing me in law and morality, in life-styles, in moral questions—all written in the last five years—for the benefit of a very puzzled people who are called to make decisions they are morally incapable of making, called only too often to step out into a wilderness without light or coal or candle. We do our best on the basis of our limited experience, relying on our memories of what mother told us, pressured by the latest television programme, wholly uncertain of the ends, and therefore inevitably of the means. When Jesus went out into the wilderness He saw that the crowds were scattered and confused, like sheep without a shepherd and, so the Gospel tells us, He taught them, making the truth of God once more available to men and women long since alienated from the temple and the synagogue. What shall I do, the young man said, to inherit eternal life? The answer was swift and uncompromising and it consisted of a recitation of the Commandments culminating in an invitation to follow Him. The Church has a responsibility to puzzled people.

6

The Church is indeed a guardian and an exponent of the law. It has inherited it; it has no option but to expound it. It is a specific remedy, so we believe, for social disorders. But if that were all, the Church in the High Street would have no more to offer than the synagogue round the corner. The law can restrain but it cannot liberate. It imposes itself upon the conscience of a man but it does not enable him to respond to it with love and joy. It is a threat, not a promise; a necessary barrier perhaps but not an open door. So on the basis of the New Testament writings the Church is able to proclaim what it is pleased to call a Gospel—good news. The good news is that Jesus, Himself the exponent of the law, became the victim of the law, condemned unjustly indeed but condemned under a genuine law of God which forbade the giving of divine honours to any but God alone. Jesus, under the law, was a blasphemer and it was for this offence that He was condemned in the Sanhedrin.

But in a curious "exchange" the law lost its power over Him; He fulfilled it wholly, perfectly—and rose triumphant from the death to which the law had consigned Him.

Thereafter His followers, whilst remaining for the greater part obedient to the law, found liberation for themselves and a new consciousness of power and adequacy. They assumed the easy yoke of Christ—in point of fact a more demanding yoke in that it required submission of the heart rather than mere external obedience. They were enabled—and the evidence of it is irresistible in the pages of the New Testament—to conquer adverse powers, to triumph over handicaps, to do the will of God joyfully and without reserve, not as of compulsion but of a discovery that God intended their good, prescribed their path, held their hands and taught them to walk in the new way. It was the wilderness experience over again but without grumbling or dissension or anxiety. They were free men, rejoicing in a power they had never before experienced. There is a well-rehearsed opinion that St. Matthew's Gospel and the Epistle of James and the Pastoral Epistles represent a backward step, alien to that earlier experience of freedom. But no—the difference is not between those who obey the law and those who ignore it but between those who suffer the law as a heavy unwelcome burden and those who rejoice in the easy yoke of Christ. At least it can be said of those early Christians that they were not puzzled people. They walked with confidence and even *élan* in a very dangerous wilderness indeed, their eyes on the Promised Land, their feet on a sure way. To them the law of God, with whatever qualifications, was part of the good news; the Sermon on the Mount was a reliable prescription for life and the private instructions to the disciples a rich source of wisdom. We who proclaim the whole Gospel had better see to it that it is whole—that we bring forth from our treasure things new and old for the moral and spiritual enrichment of those who hear us. Perhaps it is the moral dilemma, not necessarily the moral collapse, which now reveals to a man his need of the Gospel.

7

The author of Genesis or, as we shall have to say, the man responsible for the final form of the book, produced a literary and theological masterpiece. The language still reverberates in our minds and the imagery is now deeply lodged in the

minds of Western man. Modern novelists, musicians, poets
and artists have made use of it or found themselves in willing
subjection to it—Golding, Muir, Epstein, Camus, Mann,
Britten. If I set my mind to it I could produce a list five times
as long. Part of its power resides in the sheer range of the
author's imagination. He dares to set the origins of Israel
against nothing less than a cosmic background. Most of us
would have been satisfied with the prehistoric or the primeval, satisfied to observe how Israel's peculiar destiny arose
from the moral chaos which is so clearly etched in the early
chapters of Genesis. That would have been sufficient, surely,
to account for Israel's historic role as a guardian of God's
law. Need we go further back than Sodom or Gomorrah or
Babel to explain Sinai? There is not simply a geographical
but a theological propinquity between these four places. But
the author is not satisfied until he has shown that a peculiar
role of Israel arises not just within an historic but within a
cosmic setting. So behind the prehistoric and the primeval he
discerns the creation of the world and the origins of the
universe. The phrase "law and order" has an unfortunate
sound in many people's ears but it is law and order which the
author discerns behind the changing, the transient, the
seemingly unpredictable phenomena of the world. The God
who gave the law commanded also the stars and set them in
their courses. The God who guided His little flock through
the wilderness presides over the universe. I quote in Today's
English Version (Good News Bible) Psalm 148, deeply
imbued with the spirit of Genesis:

> Praise the LORD from heaven,
> you that live in the heights above.
> Praise him, all his angels,
> all his heavenly armies.
>
> Praise him, sun and moon;
> praise him, shining stars.
> Praise him, highest heavens,
> and the waters above the sky.
>
> Let them all praise the name of the LORD!
> He commanded, and they were created;

by his command they were fixed in
their places for ever,
and they cannot disobey.

Praise the LORD from the earth,
sea-monsters and all ocean depths;
lightning and hail, snow and clouds,
strong winds that obey his command.

Praise him, hills and mountains,
fruit-trees and forests;
all animals, tame and wild,
reptiles and birds.

Praise him, kings and all peoples,
princes and all other rulers;
girls and young men,
old people and children too.

Let them all praise the name of the LORD!
His name is greater than all others;
his glory is above earth and heaven.
He made his nation strong,
so that all his people praise him—
the people of Israel, so dear to him.

Praise the LORD!

Observe how close in the psalmist's mind is the connection
between the law which governs the universe and the law
which governs the Chosen People. There is a "violent
universe" and a "restless earth", the author of Genesis would
agree, but he suggests that at the end of time the earth and the
heavens, men and societies, will all partake of one great
cosmic "order" and God shall be all-in-all. On this view,
chaos in society is no more than another expression of chaos
in the natural order. The violent waves that wash up on our
social scene are but the consequences of far-off events in the
cosmic scene, just as our holiday beaches in Pembrokeshire
some three years ago were subjected to a violent battering in
consequence of a typhoon on the other side of the Atlantic

some three thousand miles away. In society, therefore, we see the same process at work—chaos being overcome in the interests of order. That is why the author of Genesis moves straight from the tohu-bohu (or chaos) of the world of nature to the tohu-bohu (or chaos) of the world of men. Adam and Eve succumb to shame, Cain murders Abel, the flood carries all the wicked away, and, in its supreme expression of disorder, the Tower of Babel collapses in a heap of dust, men are scattered all over the face of the earth, divided by language and custom and incapable of living in harmony with each other. It is against this background that God "chooses" a people who are to represent His purpose of order in the world. This is heady stuff; I am not asking you to believe, but simply to observe it—and to wonder at the breath-taking audacity of the man who could subsume the whole created order under the history of an unimportant middle-east clan. The Church then, whether it be the old Israel or the new, is not just a guardian of the law; it is a representative of it. The stately liturgy of a great cathedral, the mighty theological structures of a Thomas Aquinas or a Karl Barth, the soaring arches of some ancient abbey, the architectonic music of a Johann Sebastian Bach, alike proclaim the principle of order. Through the whole created universe the writ of God runs— He commanded and it was made. The Church is not to be regarded as just a human institution, the product of a particular culture likely to perish with that culture, but as the representative of a certain principle of life without which we can scarcely live at all.

The Individual

8
The Jew

Any Jewish reader who happens upon this book will have found in it material thoroughly familiar to him, but he will have found also that same material viewed from a disconcertingly different angle from the one he is used to. He will be reminded also of the curious irony that the Commandments delivered to his ancestors at Sinai and the staple diet of his people for three thousand years, have become the property of a world-wide fellowship often inimical to his faith and sometimes, alas, a violent persecutor of it. This world-wide fellowship was created by two men of his own race—Saul of Tarsus and Jesus of Nazareth, representing between them both the Diaspora and the Palestinian traditions of Israel. He has, if he is to remain a Jew by religion, no option but to regard these two men as seriously mistaken and indeed perverters of his ancestral faith. But I ask my Jewish reader to observe that Paul and Jesus were Jews; both of them were well instructed in the law, both of them commanded a wide hearing amongst their own people—and no one could doubt the sincerity of their belief in God, the Lord of Israel. I have, I hope, shown that neither of them disparaged the role of Israel in the world or the Sacred Scriptures which were entrusted to them. In the content and style of their utterances they were not markedly different from the prophets before them, impatient with the formality into which Jewish religion had slipped, and eager to renew the faith, as they supposed it to be, of their fathers. They were sent to the lost sheep of the House of Israel—in Palestine and in the Diaspora. Furthermore, persuasive voices have been raised amongst both Jewish and Christian scholars intent on showing that Jesus' teaching was not entirely without parallel amongst contemporary Rabbis. Much, for example, of what Jesus said can, we are told, be paralleled in the Rabbinic writings of the period immediately before and after the beginning of the Christian era. For many years it was possible to regard the Christians as a sect within Judaism and they were in fact so regarded by the Roman authorities. Thus, however far the Jewish reader may have to go before he could admit to himself that Jesus of Nazareth was the Messiah for whom his race was waiting, he could begin by concentrating on the issues raised in this book regarding the law. He does not have to be a Christian to recognise in Jesus a gifted, persuasive and radical exponent of the law, making it available to the poor, rescuing it from the professional, breathing into it new life and reminding its guardians of their responsibility before God for sharing it with the world at large. He does not have to be a Christian either to be convinced that the law is for all mankind; that is implicit in his own age-long faith. Jew and Christian could at least stand together in believing that the law in its essentials is a loving gift of God to every society not just to Jewish society. This is what some of his forefathers believed when they translated the Torah into Greek and encompassed heaven and earth to make a single proselyte.

9

The Christian

The Christian will perhaps view this book with a certain ambivalence. The argument will, I hope, have been convincing—that the law is a gift of God to be viewed not as a burden but as a resource and authoritative over all—Jew, Christian, Humanist. But he will in greater or lesser degree feel the tension which Paul felt when he struggled within himself to retain a place for the law under the influence of a dynamic experience of the spirit and to retain a place for the spirit under the overarching, undergirding law which sustains everything in heaven and earth. He will acknowledge that law is essential to the enjoyment of freedom in any kind of society we would conceivably imagine. But is there for him as a person any freedom under the law? Is he required as a child of God, saved through Christ and empowered, so he believes, by the Spirit, to live still under the shadow of Sinai, to submit to the categorical imperatives of the Decalogue? Put it another way—can he dance before the ark? I always observe that an architect appears to do his best work when he has perforce to operate within a restricted site. Give him a field and he builds a monster; give him a narrow place and he can build a masterpiece. One of the most successful vicarages in the diocese of York was made out of a bottle factory. Freedom does not mean the freedom to do anything, but the freedom to do something superlatively well within the restrictions imposed by our own physical and mental nature. The will of God, as expressed in the Commandments, is not an iron determinism which conditions every act and prescribes every objective, but ordains limits, and because of which the individual may be gloriously free. Jesus of Nazareth, the Son of God, lived out His life within the exceedingly narrow geographical boundaries of Israel, within the narrow mental boundaries of contemporary culture and within the boundaries prescribed by a seemingly restrictive moral code. "If any man therefore sets aside even the least of the law's demands and teaches others to do the same, he will have the lowest place in the kingdom of Heaven, whereas anyone who keeps the law and teaches others so, will stand high in the kingdom of Heaven" (Matthew 5: 19). Paul, confronted by the implacable opposition of his own people, would have had every cause to break with the traditions of his fathers but he could not find it in his heart to do so. Fuelled by his astounding vision for the conversion of the Gentiles he had to learn for himself the hard lesson—that he and they would have to learn to operate within certain moral limits which perhaps in the first flush of enthusiasm he had believed to be otiose. The Promised Land still lay ahead; the Son of Man did not return and there were a few years yet to live in the wilderness, the other side of Sinai indeed, but short of Jordan. He was surely right. The one who spoke to him on the Damascus road was the one who enthroned in His own person the law of God—infinitely refined, radically interpreted, but still the law of God. It is a sure instinct, therefore, which claims a place in the 1662 Prayer Book for the Decalogue and perhaps surprisingly ensured its presence in the Series Three Communion Service as well. For those not familiar with it I quote the Commandments as they are provided in the Series Three version:

> Our Lord Jesus Christ said, If you love me, keep my commandments: happy are those who hear the word of God and keep it. Hear then these commandments which God has given to his people, and take them to heart.
> I am the Lord your God: you shall have no other gods but me.
> You shall love the Lord your God with all your heart, with all your soul, with all your mind, and with all your strength.

You shall not make for yourself any idol.
God is spirit, and those who worship him must worship in spirit and in truth.

You shall not dishonour the name of the Lord your God.
You shall worship him with reverence and awe.

Remember the Lord's day and keep it holy.
Christ is risen from the dead; set your minds on things that are above, not on things that are on the earth.
Honour your father and mother.
Live as servants of God: honour all men; love the brotherhood.

You shall not commit murder.
Do not nurse anger against your brother; overcome evil with good.

You shall not commit adultery.
Know that your body is a temple of the Holy Spirit.

You shall not steal.
You shall work honestly and give to those in need.

You shall not be a false witness.
Let everyone speak the truth.

You shall not covet anything which belongs to your neigbour.
Remember the words of the Lord Jesus: It is more blessed to give than to receive. Love your neighbour as yourself, for love is the fulfilling of the law.

Moses is there indeed, but he has yielded pride of place to the Law-giver Himself. The law to which the Christian yields, in glad obedience, is the law as it is radicalised, deepened, heightened and enlarged in the mind and on the lips of Christ. It sets the boundaries within which we may freely walk, it makes our dangerous liberty bearable.

10
The Humanist

The Humanist may be surprised to find himself on parade in this strange company. But he is there because whilst he may react adversely to the biblical framework within which this book is set, he may yet assent to the possibility that the conclusion of the argument is sound. The humanist, in line with his convictions about the dignity and autonomy of man, will agree that one man's freedom is likely to depend on the extent to which the other man's freedom is in some way restrained. No freedom is possible when men are free to steal, covet, murder, to their hearts' content. But the problem will be to find a locus of authority for any system of law to which he is expected to submit. Is it just the authority of the party in power, or the will of the dictator, or the mind of the majority, or the composite tradition of the race? If I am to use his terms I am saying that it is the composite tradition of the race, given varying forms in varying cultures and authoritatively articulated in the law given to Israel. The humanist does not have to believe in the theophany on Sinai, nor to accord to Jesus or to Paul any authority greater than he would accord to other great men, but he would have to take seriously the strange persistence which maintained the law in the mind of Israel, and the strange historical process which has preserved the tradition of Israel and made that law available for all mankind through the Christian Church. That calls for explanation. I have offered one which, for a variety of reasons, I find convincing. The humanist is free to offer his own explanation, but whatever it is he will have to make room somewhere, somehow, for the recorded experiences of Israel in the wilderness. Sinai is part of the landscape. It is there, and the lightnings can still be seen and the thunders can still be heard. We owe our freedoms, such as they are, more than we sometimes suppose, to the law which Moses brought down from the mountain. If there is to be any freedom it will have to be freedom under the law.

There will be many a humanist, as indeed many a Christian and a Jew, who would echo Wordsworth's words in his "Ode to Duty":

Me this unchartered freedom tires;
I feel the weight of chance-desires;

It seems that we need the sound of the trumpet in the morning.

Index of Authors

Index of Biblical Quotations